AF269636

The Saint's Advantage by
Christ's Ascension and
Coming Again from Heaven

Soli Deo Gloria Publications
An imprint of Reformation Heritage Books
3070 29th St. SE
Grand Rapids, MI 49512
616-977-0889
orders@heritagebooks.org
www.heritagebooks.org

Printed in the United States of America
22 23 24 25 26 27/10 9 8 7 6 5 4 3 2 1

Library of Congress Cataloging-in-Publication Data

Names: Love, Christopher, 1618-1651, author. | Pederson, Randall J., 1975- editor.
Title: The Saint's advantage by Christ's ascension and coming again from heaven / Christopher Love ; edited by Randall J. Pederson.
Description: Grand Rapids, Michigan : Soli Deo Gloria Publications, an imprint of Reformation Heritage Books, [2022]
Identifiers: LCCN 2022013770 (print) | LCCN 2022013771 (ebook) | ISBN 9781601789433 (hardcover) | ISBN 9781601789440 (epub)
Subjects: LCSH: Bible. John, XIV, 4—Criticism, interpretation, etc. | Second Advent. | Jesus Christ—Ascension. | BISAC: RELIGION / Christian Living / Spiritual Growth | RELIGION / Christian Theology / Christology
Classification: LCC BS2615.52 .L68 2022 (print) | LCC BS2615.52 (ebook) | DDC 226.5/06—dc23/eng/20220524
LC record available at https://lccn.loc.gov/2022013770
LC ebook record available at https://lccn.loc.gov/2022013771

The Saint's Advantage by Christ's Ascension and Coming Again from Heaven

Christopher Love

Edited by
Randall J. Pederson

Soli Deo Gloria Publications
An imprint of Reformation Heritage Books
Grand Rapids, Michigan

CONTENTS

EDITOR'S PREFACE

Christopher Love (1618–1651) was a Welsh Presbyterian author and pastor who was executed during the English Civil War.[1] He was born into a middle-class family and converted to Christianity when he was fifteen, having had a transformative religious experience on hearing a sermon by the English Independent William Erbury.[2] Soon after his conversion, Love became a strict Puritan—against his father's wishes—but was able to get enough support from his family to study for the ministry at Oxford University. While a student, Love had the reputation of being somber, downtrodden, and melancholic, but he eventually found relief and was better enabled to console those who suffered similarly.[3]

---

1. For more on Love's life, see E. C. Vernon, "Love, Christopher." In *Oxford Dictionary of National Biography*. Oxford University Press, 2004; online ed., 2022. https://10.1093/ref:odnb/17038; and Joel R. Beeke and Randall J. Pederson, *Meet the Puritans: A Guide to Modern Reprints* (Grand Rapids: Reformation Heritage Books, 2006), 396–400. The only book-length biography of Love to be published is Don Kistler, *A Spectacle unto God: The Life and Death of Christopher Love* (Morgan, Pa.: Soli Deo Gloria, 1994).

2. Alec Ryrie, *Being Protestant in Reformation Britain* (New York: Oxford University Press, 2013), 436–37. Ryrie notes that Love's father, to prevent his son from further despondency, locked him in his room to prevent him from attending sermons. Love, however, was determined and would escape to satisfy his thirst for the word preached.

3. See, for instance, Love's *The Dejected Soul's Cure* (London, 1657), a posthumous collection of seventeen sermons on spiritual comfort. The topic of religious

In 1639 Love became a chaplain to John Warner, the sheriff of London, and held religious services at his estate.[4] It was here that he met Mary Stone, daughter of a wealthy London merchant; he eventually married her in 1645 at St. Giles-in-the-Fields Church in London. He had five children with Mary, though two did not survive infancy.[5] Their marriage was one of deep, mutual affection and love, evinced by the letters they shared during Love's later imprisonment.[6]

In 1640 Love, along with several other prominent clergymen, refused to subscribe the Laudian Canons—a collection of rules and regulations for conducting worship, including the so-called et cetera oath that most Puritans found offensive—and was consequently deprived of holy orders by William Juxton, the bishop of London, who later offered last rites to Charles I on the scaffold. There were increasing tensions between the reformist wing in the English Church and those who fought for the Establishment.

---

melancholy in early modern England remains an underexplored field of study, and though a few important books have been published in recent years, more work needs to be done, especially since the subject was common to the Puritan experience and contributed to a thriving book industry. For scholarly treatments that deal with this subject broadly, see Jeremy Schmidt, *Melancholy and the Care of the Soul: Religion, Moral Philosophy and Madness in Early Modern England* (Aldershot: Ashgate Publishing, 2007); Mary Ann Lund, *Melancholy, Medicine and Religion in Early Modern England: Reading* The Anatomy of Melancholy (Cambridge: Cambridge University Press, 2010); and Willem J. op 't Hof, "Puritan Emotions in Seventeenth-Century Dutch Piety," in *Puritanism and Emotion in the Early Modern World*, ed. Alec Ryrie and Tom Schwanda (London: Palgrave Macmillan, 2016), 213–40.

4. Warner was a well-known Puritan merchant and politician. Robert Brenner, *Merchants and Revolution: Commercial Change, Political Conflict, and London's Overseas Traders, 1550–1653* (London: Verso, 2003), 310.

5. Michael P. Winship, *Hot Protestants: A History of Puritanism in England and America* (New Haven, Conn.: Yale University Press, 2019), 128.

6. See Mary Love, *Love's Letters, His and Hers, to Each Other, a Little Before His Death* (London, 1651), which includes Love's last letter to his wife written the day of his death. Among a myriad of practical counsels, Love advises her, "Keep under a sound orthodox and soul-searching ministry" (p. 4).

Love sought ordination in Scotland from the presbytery there but was denied because he did not have a formal call to pastor a church. When he returned to London, he attacked the Book of Common Prayer and spoke against various ceremonies that he believed were vestiges of the past, but this got him into legal trouble, and he was imprisoned for a time.

In 1642 Love was appointed chaplain to the regiment of John Venn, a member of Parliament and governor of Windsor Castle. Love lived in Venn's house for two and a half years and had a favorable influence on Venn's daughter, Anne, who kept a diary detailing her religious experiences and the impression Love made on her.

Love was ordained as a Presbyterian in 1645, when the House of Lords allowed the Westminster Assembly to start ordaining clergy.[7] On January 30, 1645, Love preached a controversial sermon, "England's Distemper Having Division and Error as Cause," in which he warned Parliament not to compromise for the sake of peace and was put on house arrest but later released. In 1646 Love preached before the House of Commons and urged Parliament to purge the army of heretics, those who were believed to be too radical in their views and thus a threat to the country. He disputed William Dell, a radical Parliamentarian and alleged antinomian, on

---

7. There is some confusion in the literature as to whether Love was a formal member of the Westminster Assembly. George Gillespie noted that Love's name was "superadded" later, though Love is never referred to in any of the debates or journals of the proceedings. William Hetherington, a nineteenth-century chronicler, called Love a "superadded divine"—that is, one who was called, among others, to fill seats left vacant in the assembly because of death or other reasons. Chad Van Dixhoorn does not list Love as a divine in his monumental work, *The Minutes and Papers of the Westminster Assembly*, 1643–1653, 5 vols. (New York: Oxford University Press, 2012). While Love's status as a Westminster divine is uncertain, what is certain is that Love had no formative or influential role in the assembly or its debates. Cf. George Gillespie, *Notes of Debates and Proceedings of the Assembly of Divines and Other Commissioners at Westminster, February 1644 to January 1645*, ed. David Meek (Edinburgh: Robert Ogle and Oliver and Boyd, 1846), xi; and W. M. Hetherington, *History of the Westminster Assembly of Divines* (New York: Mark H. Newman, 1843), 98.

the Commons floor, which, at the time, was a break in custom and reveals the seriousness with which Love took the threat of English radicals, especially on millenarian teachings.

When the English civil wars broke out, Love sided with the royalists, along with numerous London Presbyterians.[8] He opposed those who fought for religious toleration because he feared that the rise of sectaries would cause irreparable harm to the English Church and Commonwealth. Moreover, there were disturbing developments within the army that alarmed conservative Presbyterians like Love: the rise of the so-called Fifth Monarchists and other radicals who not only believed in the imminent millennial reign of Christ but also felt that military and political action should be used to bring it about. Though Love had earlier opposed the bishops and ceremonies, he now considered the sectaries to be more dangerous. He fought for a more moderate tone and tried to stem the radical ideology then spreading through English society. Love's posthumous publication, *The Saint's Advantage*, portions of which were likely preached during this time, was in part a polemic against the millennial fervor infecting Independents and radicals in Parliament. Love argued that Christ's second coming would be to judge the world, not to set up an earthly reign, whether a thousand years or otherwise, as those freshly inspired by the downfall of the monarchy had hoped.[9]

---

8. See Elliot Vernon, *London Presbyterians and the British Revolutions, 1638–64* (Manchester, UK: Manchester University Press, 2021); Tai Liu, *Puritan London: A Study of Religion and Society in the City Parishes* (Newark: University of Delaware Press, 1986). Liu calls Love "the only true martyr for the Presbyterian cause during the revolutionary period" (67).

9. Stella P. Revard, "Milton and Millenarianism: From the Nativity Ode to Paradise Regained," in *Milton and the Ends of Time*, ed. Juliet Cummins (Cambridge: Cambridge University Press, 2003), 49–51; and Bryan W. Ball, *A Great Expectation: Eschatological Thought in English Protestantism to 1660* (Leiden: Brill, 1975), 30–31. See also Bernard Capp, *The Fifth Monarchy Men: A Study in Seventeenth-Century English Millenarianism* (London: Faber & Faber, 1972). The Scots and the English initially fought against the monarchy but diverged when

Sometime before 1647, Love was appointed to a parish church in Aldersgate and later pastored the vestry of St. Lawrence Jewry, London. As a fiery Presbyterian, Love spent the rest of his life fighting for the Presbyterian cause and for spiritual reformation in the city. In 1649 he was acquitted of a charge of seditious preaching but became entangled with other zealous Presbyterians who were conspiring to restore Charles II, then in exile, to the English throne. Love, along with other Presbyterians in the city, had opposed the execution of Charles I, feared what impact regicide would have on the Commonwealth, and believed the monarchy to be the best path of subduing English sectaries. For a time, the plotters met in Love's house and conferred how to get Scotland to support their cause. Known as "Love's plot" for Love's seeming role in the affair, the conspirators were eventually caught, brought to trial, and, in the case of Love, sentenced to death on the scaffold, a rare form of punishment for a clergyman, and rarer still in that just a decade earlier it would have been unheard of for Puritans to kill Puritans.[10]

During his brief imprisonment, Love wrote several letters to his wife that were later published as *Love's Letters*. His wife, in turn, wrote a biography of her husband, "The Life of Mr. Christopher Love," which has never been published.[11]

Fourteen days before his execution, Love wrote in defense of his actions. He criticized his sentence as unjust, declared his innocence, and reaffirmed that his life was in God's hands, the only One who

---

it came to regicide. The English army, inspired by millenarianism, believed they were ushering in the millennial reign of Christ, whereas the Scots were influenced more by doctrinal fidelity and upholding the Solemn League and Covenant. See Glenn A Moots, *Politics Reformed: The Anglo-American Legacy of Covenant Theology* (Columbia: University of Missouri Press, 2010), 94–98.

10. P. J. Klemp, *The Theatre of Death: Rituals of Justice from the English Civil Wars to the Restoration* (Newark: University of Delaware Press, 2016), 204; and Winship, *Hot Protestants*, 115.

11. Mary Love's manuscript was never published. There are two extant copies; one is housed in Dr. Williams's Library, and the other, an incomplete copy, is in the British Library.

had the right to cut his life and ministry short.[12] He had pledged to God to reform the Church of England and not to tear down that church as others had done. Attempts were made by Love's friends to secure his freedom, including a direct petition to Cromwell (who, at the time, was engaged in a campaign in Scotland), but they were ineffective, as were the petitions of Love's wife.[13] Love was executed on the scaffold at Tower-hill on Tuesday, August 22, 1651. His last words were, "Blessed be God, I am full of joy, and peace in believing; I lie down with a world of comfort, as if I were to lie down in my bed.... I shall rest in Abraham's bosom, and in the embraces of the Lord Jesus." In his last letter to Mary, he referred to his execution as "the day of my glorification."[14]

Thomas Manton, a friend of Love's and a fellow minister, had attended him on the scaffold and had given him his cloak as a sign of respect. Three days later Manton preached a brief sermon at Love's funeral, despite threats from Cromwell's soldiers that they would shoot him. For a time, Love's execution successfully quashed Presbyterian pulpit resistance to Cromwell's regime.[15]

Love refused to compromise his principles and lost his life for it. He was a firm supporter of the monarchy, believed religious

---

12. Christopher Love, *A Clear and Necessary Vindication of the Principles and Practices of Me, Christopher Love* (London, 1651).

13. Mary Love's petitions were later published as *Love's Name Lives: or, A Publication of Diverse Petitions Presented by Mistress Love to the Parliament in Behalf of Her Husband* (London, 1651).

14. Christopher Love, *Mr. Love's Speech Made on the Scaffold on Tower-hill, August 22, 1651* (London, 1651), 16; *Love's Letters*, 6.

15. Elliot Vernon, "Presbyterians in the English Revolution," in *The Oxford History of Protestant Dissenting Traditions*, ed. John Coffey (New York: Oxford University Press, 2020), 1:68. There was a brief time, a few weeks before the restoration of the monarchy in 1660, that Presbyterianism was restored to ascendency, but the resolution fell apart, and most of the ministers who had influence under Cromwell lost their positions in the Restoration church. Ann Hughes, "The Cromwellian Church," in *The Oxford History of Anglicanism*, vol. 1, *Reformation and Identity, c. 1520–1662*, ed. Anthony Milton (Oxford: Oxford University Press, 2017), 455–56.

toleration to be a web with spiders lurking in the shadows, and preached wherever possible against sectaries and theologies that sought to establish an earthly kingdom. His actual involvement in the plot that took his life is uncertain and may never fully be known. He maintained his innocence against charges of treason and wrote that his guilt was to entertain guests and oversee fasts where letters were read in support of the king. In the immediate aftermath of Love's execution, there was an intense storm in London that Love's supporters in the city interpreted as a sign of God's displeasure over the execution. Nehemiah Wallington, a Puritan chronicler, noted that for years afterward, fires and other disasters scourging the city were similarly interpreted.[16]

Love's written works, many of which were hastily published in the years following his execution, cover a broad range of subjects and include writings on spiritual comfort to sermons on the state of the unconverted to a treatise on heaven and hell. In addition to English printings, several of Love's works were translated into Dutch, including his scaffold speech.[17] To this day, Love is remembered for his pithy, winsome expressions and solid exegesis of the biblical text.

The present edition of Christopher Love's *The Saint's Advantage* is a slightly edited and partially modernized edition. For ease of reading, the text has been broken up into chapters and given chapter titles. Initially, the text, as originally published, posed many

---

16. Margarette Lincoln, *London and the 17th Century: The Making of the World's Greatest City* (New Haven, Conn.: Yale University Press, 2021), 88; and Vernon, *London Presbyterians and the British Revolutions*, 232–35.

17. The translation of Love's works into Dutch was spearheaded by two Dutch reformers, Jacobus Koelman and Hendrick Versteegh. Helmer J. Helmers, *The Royalist Republic: Literature, Politics, and Religion in the Anglo-Dutch Public Sphere, 1639–1660* (Cambridge: Cambridge University Press, 2015), 103–4. For more on how Love was revived and translated in Holland, see W. J. op 't Hof and F. W. Huisman, eds., *Nederlandse liefde voor Christopher Love (1618–1651): Studies over het vertaalde werk van een presbyteriaanse puritein* (Amstelveen: Eon Pers, 2013).

challenges. It was printed as a seamless whole with relatively few breaks for the reader. The content, which consists of ten sermons that Love preached—the day, place, and hour unknown—was based on a hearer's sermon notes ("taken from the mouth of the reverend Author")[18] and was rushed into print to satisfy a craving for Love's works. This first printing of 1652/1653, the Cranford edition (being printed by James Cranford, a Presbyterian pastor and licenser for divinity books), had questionable authenticity and was published with numerous typographical errors.[19] A few years later, Edmund Calamy, Love's executor and the only person authorized by Love's wife to publish her husband's authentic works, revised the manuscript and compared it line by line with Love's handwritten notes. The result was that passages presumed not to be from Love or that could not be confirmed to be Love's words were excised, and those left out of the first printing but found in Love's notes were inserted. The result was the authorized Calamy text of 1657, which this new edition is based on.[20] Though Calamy took greater care with the text, it was clear from the outset that it still retained many hurdles for modern audiences, not least of which was how the text flowed into one lengthy composition.

Another issue was to what extent the text should be modernized. Readers today are becoming more accustomed to full modernizations that use more recent English Bible translations, updated spellings, and the replacement of obscure words. But given the aim to produce an accessible but authentic reproduction of the original,

---

18. James Cranford, "To the Reader," in Christopher Love, *The Soul's Cordial* (London, 1652), sig. A4–5.

19. Edmund Calamy, "To the Christian Reader," in Christopher Love, *The Penitent Pardoned* (London, 1657), sig. A3–4.

20. Though the Calamy edition seems to have been printed only once in the seventeenth century, it nevertheless had a degree of popularity. Oliver Heywood owned a copy and lent it out, never to get it back. Andrew Cambers, *Godly Reading: Print, Manuscript and Puritanism in England, 1570–1720* (Cambridge: Cambridge University Press, 2011), 129.

it was decided to update spelling without paraphrase or substitution of phrases. Endings have been generally kept (*hath* remains), and pronouns for deity are capitalized. Where needed, arabic numerals have been inserted in places where confusion might result; in the original, it was common for a series of "firsts" to occur in proximity, thus creating a perfect storm for puzzlement.

Punctuation has been updated where possible, though at times it may seem irregular, given the free hand of early modern typesetters, who sometimes inserted commas to slow down a reader and sometimes omitted them to speed up a reader. Finally, a few explanatory notes were inserted to clarify a word used or to shed light on a person or book that Love is citing. These were purposefully kept to a minimum so as not to distract the reader from the main text.

Overall, the editorial philosophy was to produce an edition that is faithful to the original but does not burden the reader with outdated typography or the strangeness of early modern print. It is hoped that this new edition of *The Saint's Advantage* will not only reach an audience already familiar with Love's works but will help to introduce new readers to Love's insight and exposition of the Bible.

CHAPTER 1

Five Fundamental Doctrines of Religion

And if I go and prepare a place for you, I will come again, and receive you unto myself; that where I am, there ye may be also.
— JOHN 14:3

This chapter, out of which my text is taken, is counted famous by most interpreters because in it begins the legacy that Christ gives, and the last will and testament that Christ made when He was to leave the world. This will and testament of Christ's begins in this 14th chapter and continues to the 18th chapter of this book. The scope and drift of this chapter is to comfort His disciples, both against their fears of persecution in the world, as also against their sorrows, upon this consideration that Christ was shortly to leave this world. And Christ here mentions many comfortable considerations to fence them against their fears, for this much troubled them. It went ill with them when Christ was with them, and they thought it would have been worse with them when He was gone, and He encourages them therefore by these arguments.

First, He says, "I am but going to My Father's house." And in the 28th verse of this chapter, He says, "Ye have heard how I said unto you, I go away, and come again unto you. If ye loved me, ye would rejoice, because I said, I go unto the Father: for my Father is greater than I."

Secondly, He would not have them troubled because of His departure; because, says He, "I do not intend to go to My Father alone but intend to have all [of] you with Me, though you shall not go with Me now. Though you shall not die with Me now, though you shall not go to heaven with Me now, yet you shall be with Me another day, 'In my Father's house there are many mansions.' I do not intend to go to heaven alone, for there is room for you as well as for Me, and room for every believer in the world." Heaven first is a *mansion*, a place which notes a duration of saints in heaven. Heaven is not a moveable place but a *mansion*, an abiding place.

Again, there are many mansions in heaven. There is room enough for Christ, for His eleven apostles, and room enough for all the believers in the world. It notes the largeness and amplitude of heaven. Hebrews 11:12: "Therefore sprang there even of one, and him as good as dead, so many as the stars of the sky in multitude, and as the sand, which is by the sea shore innumerable." And besides these there is an innumerable company of angels (Heb. 12:22). To this add Revelation 7:9: "a great multitude, which no man could number, of all nations, and kindreds, and people, and tongues." You have here also the duration and continuance implied. The word is here not our tent or tabernacle but our *mansion*.

Thirdly, from the certainty of it. It is no poetical fiction. These are no hyperbolic expressions, as follows in the text: "If it were not so, I would have told you." Christ does not speak more than there is. If there had been no such thing, Christ would not have said so much. It is as if He should say, "I do not feed you with false hopes of a utopian happiness, as the devil deals by his, whom he brings into a fool's paradise."

Fourthly, from the end. Say the disciples, "But Lord, Thou art going to Thy Father's house, and what shall become of us?" Therefore, Christ comforts them and says, "I go to prepare a place for you"; as if He should have said, "I go to heaven to make ready heaven for you until you die." As Grotius[1] observes, the phrase is borrowed from a company of travelers which send one man before as a harbinger to provide the inn, and take up rooms, and make provision ready for them until they come. So Jesus Christ has gone to heaven that He might be as a harbinger to take up heaven for you, to take up room for you in heaven.

Fifthly, He comforts them by a promise of His coming again, verse 3: "And if I go and prepare a place for you, I will come again."

Sixthly, by this, that he will receive us to Himself, verse 3. "And receive you unto myself, that where I am, there ye may be also," and we shall ever be with the Lord.

I shall explain the phrases when I come to handle them as they lie in order.

This text contains in it the most material and fundamental points of all doctrines of Christianity, as,

First, the great doctrine of Christ's bodily ascension into heaven, "If I go" (Doctrine 1).

Secondly, the fruit and benefit of Christ's going into heaven, "I go to prepare a place for you" (Doctrine 2).

Thirdly, here is the great doctrine of Christ's second coming to judge the quick and the dead, "but I come again" (Doctrine 3).

Fourthly, here is the great doctrine of the resurrection of the body, "Christ shall come to receive them again from the dead, and all the elect with them" (Doctrine 4).

Fifthly, here is the great doctrine of that everlasting communion that the saints shall have with Christ in heaven, "that where I am, there ye may be also" (Doctrine 5).

---

1. Hugo Grotius (1583–1645), Dutch humanist philosopher and theologian whose theories of natural law had a major impact on seventeenth-century political thought. He fought for toleration and irenicism. His major work, *De Jure Belli ac Pacis* (1625), is considered one of the greatest works on international law.

The first clause, "If I go"; it is a good note that Calvin[2] has on these words, [that] this conditional particle ought to be resolved into an adverb of time, "If I go." It is not a note of dubitation,[3] if Christ should go to heaven or no, or a supposition, peradventure[4] he may go to heaven, peradventure not, but it serves for limitation of time when Christ does go to heaven. A like phrase you have [in] John 12:32: "And I, if I be lifted up from the earth, will draw all men unto me." This He spoke of what death He should die; if He be lifted on the cross, He should save many by His death. The word "if" does not note a dubitation or a supposition ("it may be," or "it may not be"), but it notes an adverb of time, "when I am lifted up," and so in my text: "And if I go and prepare a place for you, I will come again, and receive you unto myself, that where I am, there ye may be also." There is no difficulty in the first expression, "If I go and prepare a place for you," from which words there are two observations:

First, that Christ's ascension, or going up to heaven, is a ground of great comfort and advantage to all His people while they dwell here upon earth.

The second observation is from the end and benefit of His going up to heaven: "If I go, I go to prepare a place for you." That is, that the great end of Jesus Christ's going bodily to heaven is to prepare heaven for all the elect.

---

2. John Calvin (1509–1564), French Reformed theologian, biblical commentator, pastor, and leader of the Reformed movement in Geneva.

3. *dubitation*: doubt or hesitation.

4. *peradventure*: perhaps.

CHAPTER 2

Christ's Ascension to Heaven

The first doctrine [is] that Christ's ascension or going up to heaven is a ground of comfort and great advantage to all God's people while they dwell here upon earth. In the handling of this point there are three particulars:

Confirmation of Christ's Ascension

First, I shall prove it to you by Scripture that Christ has gone bodily into heaven. I prove it by these five arguments in Scripture:

1. By the types that were before the law. Enoch was translated and taken up bodily into heaven, where now he is. Genesis 5:24: "And Enoch walked with God: and he was not; for God took him." This is confirmed by the apostle, Hebrews 11:5: "By faith Enoch was translated that he should not see death; and was not found, because God had translated him: for before his translation he had this testimony, that he pleased God." And under the law, Elijah was taken up in a fiery chariot, 2 Kings 2:11: "And it came to pass, as they still went on, and talked, that, behold, there appeared a chariot of fire, and horses of fire, and parted them both asunder; and Elijah went up by a whirlwind into heaven." So Christ makes a third [example] under the gospel, [in that He was] taken up to heaven also.

2. [The] second argument to prove this doctrine is by prophecies in the Old Testament that Jesus Christ was to be taken up into heaven bodily. [There are] three prophecies, one in the 68th Psalm, [where] David prophesied of Christ in the 18th verse: "Thou hast ascended on high, &c." Now we should not have known so full that this had reference to Jesus Christ's ascension if Paul had not expounded this in Hebrews 4 and the 14th verse, "Seeing then that we have a great high priest, that is passed into the heavens, Jesus the Son of God, let us hold fast our profession." The prophecies that were long before Christ was born declared that Jesus Christ should ascend up into heaven, and in the 110th Psalm, 7th verse, "He shall drink of the brook in the way: therefore he shall lift up the head." What is that? It is spoken of Christ: "I will set Him upon my right-hand, first, He shall drink of the brook by the way. He shall cry, 'I thirst' upon the cross. He shall die and be crucified, then afterwards He shall lift up His head. He shall rise again and ascend up into heaven." [There is] a full prophecy in Daniel 7:13–14: "I saw in the night visions, and, behold, one like the Son of man came with the clouds of heaven, and came to the Ancient of days, and they brought him near before him. And there was given him dominion, and glory, and a kingdom, that all people, nations, and languages, should serve him: his dominion is an everlasting dominion, which shall not pass away, and his kingdom that which shall not be destroyed." This cannot be spoken of Christ's coming to judgment, but then the text says he shall deliver them to his Father (1 Cor. 15:24). But the coming of Christ in the clouds here is Christ's going up into heaven, as it is in Acts 1, verse 9: "And when he had spoken these things, while they beheld, he was taken up; and a cloud received him out of their sight." And thus you have it by prophecies confirmed.

3. The doctrine of Christ's going up to heaven is confirmed to you by Christ's promises. Christ upon the earth promised

that He would go up to heaven, John 6:62: "What and if ye shall see the Son of man ascend up where he was before?" In John 20:17, "Jesus saith unto her, Touch me not, for I am not yet ascended to my Father; but go to my brethren, and say unto them, I ascend unto my Father, and your Father, and to my God, and your God." Christ promised that He would ascend. John 16:5, 7: "But now I go my way to him that sent me; and none of you asketh me, Wither goest thou? …Nevertheless, I tell you the truth; It is expedient for you that I go away: for if I go not away, the Comforter will not come unto you; but if I depart, I will send him unto you." John 16:16: "A little while, and ye shall not see me: and again, a little while, and ye shall see me, because I go to the Father." I could quote you many Scriptures in which Christ promised He would go away.

4. The doctrine of Christ's going up to heaven is confirmed by the testimony of the apostles, who were eyewitnesses of Christ's ascension. Gerard[1] notes, saying, "Jesus Christ did rise invisible, none saw him rise; the Scripture tells you that the soldiers that watched were asleep, yet Christ gathers all his eleven apostles that they might be eyewitnesses of His ascension, that they saw him ascend to heaven, Acts 1:9–10, 'And when he had spoken these things, while they beheld, he was taken up; and a cloud received him out of their sight. And while they looked steadfastly towards heaven as he went up, behold, two men stood by them in white apparel.'" And so the apostle Peter, in 1 Peter 3:22, "Who is gone into heaven, and is on the right hand of God; angels and authorities and powers being made subject unto him." So Paul tells you in Ephesians 4:10: "He that descended is the same also that ascended up far above all heavens, that he might fill all things." So in

---

1. Johann Gerhard (1582–1637), Lutheran scholastic theologian and author of numerous influential treatises, such as his *Loci Communes Theologici* (1610–1622).

Hebrews 9, the author of that book tells you that Jesus Christ has not gone into the holy place but has gone into heaven itself, in verse 24, "For Christ is not entered into the holy places made with hands, which are the figures of the true; but into heaven itself, now to appear in the presence of God for us." First Tim. 3:16: "And without controversy great is the mystery of godliness: God was manifest in the flesh, justified in the Spirit, seen of angels, preached unto the Gentiles, believed on in the world, received up into glory." And in Mark 16:19: "So then after the Lord had spoken unto them, he was received up into heaven, and sat on the right hand of God." I take more pains to prove this because of what ancient heresies there have been to overthrow this great comfortable doctrine of Christ's going bodily into heaven, having our flesh in heaven this very day.

5. It may be proven by the concurrent testimonies of the angels, who were witnesses of this truth, Acts 1:10: "And while they looked steadfastly toward heaven as he went up, behold, two men stood by them in white apparel." These two men were angels; the angels gave their concurrent testimony that Jesus Christ went into heaven, and the same Jesus Christ that went shall come again. Beloved, I know not any one point in all the Bible that is so proved and strengthened as Christ's personal and bodily going up to heaven. And this much will suffice to strengthen you in the proof of the point. I lay that for the foundation because if the proof of it is not well-grounded, then the fruit of it will not be well-regarded.

Reasons for Christ's Ascension

Secondly, what is the reason that Christ must have His body and soul go up to heaven?

1. Christ in His bodily presence must go to heaven lest His disciples should be taken too much with His bodily presence and never look after the communication of His Spirit.

Therefore, they ask Christ, "Lord, when wilt Thou restore the kingdom to Israel?" They expected that Christ would take away the Roman emperor, which was a heathen, and expected that He would be king Himself. Acts 1:6: "When they therefore were come together, they asked of him, saying, Lord, wilt thou at this time restore again the kingdom to Israel?" It is for this reason, say interpreters, because the disciples should not dote on Jesus Christ, as to look on Him as a temporal king, and look on Him for a temporal kingdom but that they might look after the kingdom where He is. Therefore, Paul has a passage in 2 Corinthians 5:16: "Wherefore henceforth know we no man after the flesh: yea, though we have known Christ after the flesh, yet now henceforth know we him no more." As if he should say, "It may be those who lived in Christ's time, that knew Him according to the flesh as a lovely person." But, says Paul, "We know Him in a spiritual way, to look after heaven by Christ, to look after salvation by Christ."

2. Christ must be taken up into heaven in His body to make compensation and a recompense to Himself for His sufferings in His body. Philippians 2:8–9: "And being found in fashion as a man, he humbled himself, and became obedient unto death, even the death of the cross. Wherefore God also hath highly exalted him, and given him a name which is above every name." Therefore, God did exalt Christ and raise Him from the dead, and bring Him to heaven, because He obeyed to the death of the cross, and took on Him the form of a servant, Psalm 110, last verse, "He shall drink of the brook in the way: therefore shall he lift up the head." [The meaning is] "because Thou died and suffered, therefore Thou shalt lift up Thy head, therefore Thou shalt ascend up to heaven." Hebrews 2:9: "But we see Jesus, who was made a little lower than the angels for the suffering of death, crowned with glory and honour; that he by the grace of God should taste death for every man." For suffering of death, He

was crowned with glory and honor and translated bodily into heaven, that is a second argument.

3. Christ was taken up bodily to heaven. It was manifest to the world that Christ was God as well as man to manifest the godhead of Jesus Christ, therefore taken up bodily to heaven. Ephesians 4:9–10: "Now that he ascended, what is it but that he also descended first into the lower parts of the earth? He that descended is the same also that ascended up far above all heavens, that he might fill all things." There the apostle proves that Christ going up to heaven was an argument that Christ came down from heaven. So in John 6:62: "What and if ye shall see the Son of man ascend up where he was before?" This shows that Christ was in heaven before; therefore, He must be co-equal with God and co-eternal with God the Father. And thus you have the second point dispatched to you, showing the reasons why Jesus Christ must go bodily into heaven.

Comfort from Christ's Ascension

The third point is, what benefit and comfort is that to us that Jesus Christ is now bodily in heaven? What comfort was this to the disciples that Jesus Christ should leave them, and that He must go from them unto His Father's house? There are seven particulars that it is a great ground of comfort to all the people of God that Jesus Christ is gone bodily to heaven.

1. Christ's going to heaven bodily assures you of Christ's full triumph and complete conquest over all your spiritual enemies. This the apostle lays down as a ground of comfort upon Christ's ascension, Ephesians 4:8: "Wherefore he saith, When he ascended up on high, he led captivity captive, and gave gifts unto men." That is, the devil and sin that carried you captive; Christ by going up to heaven has led them captive, that is, has led your spiritual enemies who carried you captive. Christ alluded to the custom among the Romans that when the Roman conqueror rode to

the capital of Rome to rejoice in his victory over his enemies, the conqueror used to tie his captives to the chariot wheels. So Christ did carry His captives by His wheels, as it were. He led captivity captive. Colossians 2:15: "And having spoiled principalities and powers, he made a shew of them openly, triumphing over them in it." So that, beloved, here is one great comfort: that Christ, by going up to heaven, does manifest and declare to all the world that He has overcome the grave, death, devil, and sin.

2. Christ's going bodily to heaven is a pledge to you that Christ will one day bring your bodies to heaven. "I go to heaven that I may receive you to myself," that you may be bodily in heaven where Christ is. In John 14:19: "Yet a little while, and the world seeth me no more; but ye see me: because I live, ye shall live also." As if He should say, "Well, I must leave you, and I must go to heaven before you; but because I live in heaven, and live there bodily, you shall also live with Me in heaven with your bodies." Tertullian[2] makes this use of it to comfort the Christians in his days; says he: "Jesus Christ did carry our flesh into heaven with Him, and He is of our flesh and of our bone." Now says Tertullian, "Jesus Christ hath carried our flesh into heaven, and this is a good pledge unto us that our flesh shall be in heaven where Christ is also. Therefore, O flesh and blood, do thou rejoice, that hast possest heaven in Christ already. And Christ would be imperfect in heaven should not the bodies of believers come there also. Because He lives in heaven, you shall live there also."

3. Christ's going bodily to heaven is a ground of comfort to you because Christ is gone bodily into heaven to perform and accomplish His sacerdotal office, that is, as a high priest. He is

---

2. Quintus Septimus Florens Tertullianus (ca. 145–ca. 220), an early Christian apologist from Carthage, North Africa, known primarily for his writings defending the Christian faith.

now in heaven to perform the office of a high priest, to make intercession to God His Father on your behalf, that your sins might be pardoned, that your souls might be saved, that your bodies might be raised, and received into heaven with Him in glory, Hebrews 9:24: "For Christ is not entered into the holy places made with hands, which are the figures of the true; but into heaven itself, now to appear in the presence of God for us." Christ has entered into the very heavens that He might appear before God for us; so in Hebrews 7:26: "For such an high priest became us, who is holy, harmless, undefiled, separate from sinners, and made higher than the heavens."

It became us to have a high priest in heaven. Therefore observe, though it was a great benefit to the disciples to have Christ's bodily presence, yet Jesus Christ could never have fulfilled the office of the priesthood to make intercession for all the elect if Christ had not gone bodily into heaven. Will you observe one text in Hebrews 8:4: "For if he were on earth, he should not be a priest, seeing that there are priests that offer gifts according to the law." Christ must go to heaven, and there He is a priest; now if He were upon the earth, He could not be a priest for us; therefore, we have a great advantage by Christ going into heaven.

O beloved, then look on this as a great comfort that our Lord Jesus Christ is now in heaven in His body, flesh and blood, appearing before God, making intercession for all His people. This was typified out under the law. Exodus 28:9–12: "And thou shalt take two onyx stones, and grave on them the names of the children of Israel: Six of their names on one stone, and the other six names of the rest on the other stone, according to their birth. With the work of an engraver in stone, like the engravings of a signet, shalt thou engrave the two stones with the names of the children of Israel: thou shalt make them to be set in ouches of gold. And thou shalt put the two stones upon the shoulders of the ephod for stones of memorial unto the children of Israel: and Aaron shall bear their names before the LORD upon his two shoulders for a memorial." This is a type of Jesus Christ, our high priest, who is gone into that which is so in itself, the holy of holiest, and there He has not only the names of all the elect of God throughout the world on His breast but has them in His heart; and there He makes intercession for them to His Father. This is a third ground of comfort that they have of Christ's going bodily into heaven.

4. That Jesus Christ has gone into heaven to convey to you a fuller communication of the gifts and graces of His Spirit, which was bestowed on His people while He was upon the earth, Ephesians 4, verse 8, "Wherefore he saith, When he ascended up on high, he led captivity captive, and gave gifts unto men." It is an allusion to the Roman custom that when the conqueror rode in triumph towards the capital he did not only lead the prisoners by the chariot wheels but likewise scattered money to the spectators that saw him ride along in triumph. So the Lord Jesus Christ, having by His ascension spoiled death and the devil, thus Jesus Christ does cast His gifts unto men, dispenses His graces in a greater measure into the hearts of His people; not that we are to run into the Socinian error, because of this text they gather that before Christ's ascension into heaven there was no saving gift of the Spirit, and they ground it on that text, John 7, verses 38–39, "He that believeth on me, as the scripture hath said, out of his belly shall flow rivers of living water. (But this spake he of the Spirit, which they that believe on him should receive; for the Holy Ghost was not yet given; because that Jesus was not yet glorified.)" The Holy Ghost was not yet given because Jesus Christ was not yet glorified. But this text is not to be taken simply, then it would follow that Abraham, Isaac and Jacob had not the Spirit, and then they could not be in heaven. But the meaning is that the gifts of the Holy Ghost

in that abundant measure were not given because Christ was not yet ascended. Christ reserved the full giving of the Holy Ghost to the time of His ascension, and until He was glorified. Therefore, the apostles soon after His ascension received the Holy Ghost in a greater measure than was given to the people of old. And, beloved, not only gifts to bring you to heaven but also ministerial gifts to qualify men fit for the ministry—you are to look on this also as the fruit of Christ's ascension, Ephesians 4:10–12: "He that descended is the same also that ascended up far above all heavens, that he might fill all things. And he gave some, apostles; and some, prophets; and some, evangelists; and some, pastors and teachers; for the perfecting of the saints, for the work of the ministry, For the edifying of the body of Christ." So that you are to look upon not only your own Christian gifts, whereby God brings you to heaven, but all ministerial gifts are the fruits of Christ's going to heaven.

5. Christ is gone to heaven. It is to comfort us in this, that Christ, being bodily in heaven it might make you holy and bold, and fiducially confident whenever you come to God in prayer. When you do come to God in prayer, come to Him as one that has Jesus Christ at His right hand in heaven, presenting your prayers to God for you. Observe that comfortable advice given, Hebrews 4:14, 16: "Seeing then that we have a great high priest, that is passed into the heavens, Jesus the Son of God, let us hold fast our profession…. Let us therefore come boldly unto the throne of grace, that we may obtain mercy, and find grace to help in time of need." Jesus Christ's being in heaven should work a holy boldness in us to keep out fear and distrust when we pray; because we have a high priest that has passed into the highest heavens, Jesus, the Son of God. Who would not come boldly to the court when he knows that the king's eldest son is his friend, and is assured of his love, that he will intercede for him to his father? Jesus Christ is the king of heaven, the eldest Son, and

He is bound by office to present all our supplications and make intercession for us.

6. That Christ has gone bodily into heaven, it may be of comfort that yet He has the same relation towards a believer, which he had to them while He was upon the earth. When He was on the earth, Christ did say, "Go, tell my brethren that I am to ascend." And after He was taken up into heaven, He called them His brethren. Hebrews 2:11: "For both he that sanctifieth and they who are sanctified are all of one: for which cause he is not ashamed to call them brethren." Though Christ was crowned with glory and gone up to heaven, yet He was not ashamed to call believers brethren. Now in heaven, Christ is your God there, and Christ is your Father there; Christ is your prince there, and Christ is your friend there, and this may administer much comfort to you that Jesus Christ retains the same relation now He is in heaven that He had with you in the world; therefore, Job could speak in a vision, "I know that my redeemer liveth"; I know my kinsman lives (for so the word signifies). Christ called His disciples brothers when He was in the flesh, and so He calls them brothers now He is in heaven. Suppose you are a poor woman that marries a man that is mean and poor in the world; why suppose this man should come to the dignity of a king; it would be a great comfort to you that you who were but a beggar are now become a king's wife; so though you are mean in the world, yet Jesus Christ prefers you to be His brother.

7. Lastly, it may serve for comfort in this regard, that Christ is gone to heaven for this very purpose, to prepare heaven for you. "I go to prepare a place for you." Hebrews 6:20: "Whither the forerunner is for us entered, even Jesus, made an high priest for ever after the order of Melchisedec." Christ is our forerunner, gone to heaven for us. Christ not only died for us, but Christ went to heaven for us. Hebrews 10:19–20: "Having therefore, brethren, boldness to enter into the holiest by the blood of Jesus,

By a new and living way, which he hath consecrated for us, through the veil, that is to say, his flesh"; that is, having hopes to come to enter into heaven by the blood of Christ, through Christ's flesh as dying on the cross. And thus much be spoken for the doctrinal part of this point; the point was this, that Christ's ascension or going up bodily to heaven is a ground of great comfort to God's people while they live here upon the earth.

Instructions from Christ's Ascension

I shall now draw out instructions from some circumstances in Christ's going to heaven. There are five circumstances from which you may gather some instruction.

First, from the time when Christ left the world and ascended up to go to heaven. If you read the evangelists they will tell you it was about the thirty-third year of His age [that] He left this world and goes up to heaven. Learn this much from thence: that if Christ would leave the world in the flower of His age, a young man, then this should be fastened to the meditation of you young men, that you should not have your hearts too much glued to the world to hanker after a long life. Suppose God should take you away now in the flower of your age. Be willing and submissive, for God took Christ away so.

Secondly, you may learn somewhat from the place whence Christ did ascend. It is very observable: it was Mount Olivet, Acts 1:12: "Then returned they unto Jerusalem from the mount called Olivet, which is from Jerusalem a sabbath day's journey." Luke says it was from Bethany, Luke 24:50–51: "And he led them out as far as to Bethany, and he lifted up his hands, and blessed them. And it came to pass, while he blessed them, he was parted from them, and carried up into heaven." It is all one, but there is much of God's mind in this, of all the places in the world, Christ made choice of Bethany by Mount Olivet to go up to heaven. Beloved, the reason was because that was the place where Christ was taken when Judas came with the Scribes and Pharisees to apprehend Him. From that place He was taken to be crucified, and seeing it was from that place, He would choose that place from whence he would take his rise to go up to heaven. בטעני of ענה, "Bethany," in Hebrew signifies a house of affliction. Christ made that which was the house of His affliction that Bethany to be the place of the translation of Him into glory. I would give you thence to note that God does oftentimes make our sufferings to be inlets to our glory. So it was with Christ; from Bethany He was taken a prisoner, and from that same place He would ascend up into heaven. So if you suffer with Him, you shall also be glorified with Him. You may be carried to heaven sometime in ways of sharp afflictions; therefore, be not daunted at persecution, for the Lord makes Bethanies, the houses of our afflictions, to have a trapdoor in them to let us into our Father's mansion.

Thirdly, from the circumstance in Christ's ascension, that just as Christ ascended, He was speaking to His disciples things that appertained to the kingdom of God, and as He was blessing them, He was taken up before their eyes. Acts 1:9: "And when he had spoken these things, while they beheld, he was taken up; and a cloud received him out of their sight." While He was blessing His disciples, and while He was speaking to them of things appertaining to the kingdom of God, He was taken away. I would give you this note from thence, that when you come towards the time of your departure out of this world, make Christ your example. Christ as He was going away, He spake of things appertaining to the kingdom of God; so let your hearts be full fraught with divine contemplation. Do you leave good counsel behind you when you come to die, so that somebody may say these are the last words of a dying friend? I might extend this example of Christ, before His departure out of the world, unto masters of families, that when you come towards your end, leave good counsel behind you. Let not your speech be filled with worldly affairs, but let them be settled before; but leave good counsel with your children. Jacob when he was to die, he called all his children about him and gave good counsel unto them and blessed them. Likewise, David in 1 Chronicles 28:9: "And thou, Solomon my son, know thou the God of thy father, and serve him with a perfect heart and with a willing mind: for the LORD searcheth all hearts, and understandeth all the imaginations of the thoughts: if thou seek him, he will be found of thee; but if thou forsake him, he will cast thee off for ever." And thus we see in the instances of Isaac, and many other servants of God, Moses to Joshua when he was to die, but especially take Christ's example, that when you are to leave the world, you may have your minds possessed with nothing else but things appertaining to the kingdom of God, as Christ was.

Fourthly, there is instruction to be gathered from the manner of Christ's leaving the world, the manner was in Acts 1:9: "And when he had spoken these things, while they beheld, he was taken up; and a cloud received him out of their sight." They saw Him by degrees ascend into heaven. This must not pass our meditation, that a cloud should take Jesus Christ out of our sight. It is for a relief to your meditations, that when you see the clouds, to think that these clouds that I see hover in the heaven, they are Christ's chariot that once carried Him to heaven, and they are the chariots that shall carry Jesus Christ to judge the world. O labor to have your meditations on divine things; he went up in a cloud, [and] therefore the clouds are called God's chariots.

Fifthly, note that circumstance in Christ's ascension, that He would call all his friends about Him; it is expressly said all the eleven apostles were with him, Acts 1. And an interpreter thinks that there was an hundred and twenty with Jesus Christ, when He ascended up into heaven, and he gathered it from Acts 1:15, "And in those days Peter stood up in the midst of the disciples, and said, (the number of names together were about an hundred and twenty.)" Now learned men do think that there was an hundred and twenty that did see Jesus Christ ascend up to heaven. It is clear that there were the eleven apostles there, and if this be so, that Christ gathered about Him His friends when He was to leave the world, I gather thence that when you are drawing towards your end and departing out of the world, labor to have your friends about you so that you might give them the advice of a dying friend, and it is a great blessing to die amongst your friends. Christ before that He would go up to heaven and leave the world, He would have His friends about Him, and then He was taken up from them.

Applications of Christ's Ascension

I now come to draw out more practical application of this point. If it be so that Christ's going up bodily into heaven be a ground of such great comfort unto the people of God upon earth, the use that I shall draw shall be to deduce four doctrinal and four practical inferences from this point.

First, this point confutes the opinion of the Selucians and Hermiani,[3] who hold that Christ's body is not in heaven but that it is in the beautiful and splendid body of the sun, and they say that is the reason the sun casts such a glorious light over what the moon does. And truly this old heresy is again revived amongst us, and I have seen it in a book called *Divine Light*, when indeed it is nothing but darkness. But Christ is above the sun; Christ is above all the visible heavens. Christ sits in the third heaven, as Paul calls it; therefore, if Christ's body be gone into heaven, they are in an error.

Secondly, this point will confute those who hold that Christ's body has been on earth since His ascension into heaven. Some

---

3. See Andrew Willet, *Tetrastylon Papisticum* (1593), 88–89.

in Germany held that they were the very Christ, and thus in King Henry the Eighth's days, there was one held that he was the Christ, his side was pierced, and there was the print of nails seen in his hand. But if men say, "Lo, here is Christ," and "There is Christ," believe them not, for Christ was never on the earth since His ascension.

Thirdly, that Christ's body is now in heaven, it overthrows the doctrine of the popish religion touching transubstantiation, or the real presence, that Jesus Christ is bodily present at the sacrament; say the papists, "we bodily eat Christ's flesh and drink Christ's blood"; [they believe] that Christ is as bodily present at the sacrament as he was on the cross. If there were no other argument to overthrow this opinion but this, that the body of Christ is now in heaven, it were enough then that opinion of transubstantiation is hereby confuted. Christ's body cannot be in heaven and on earth both at one time.

Fourthly, the ascension of Christ overthrows the opinion of the Carpacratiami that hold that only His soul did go to heaven, and His body perished as others; and this cannot be, for the disciples said that they saw Christ ascend, and this must be His body, for they could not see His soul, for the soul is a spirit. Now you see the reason why I spent so much time in the morning in giving you many texts of Scripture to prove this point: because there are so many heretics that do oppugn this doctrine of Christ's ascension.

Deductions from Christ's Ascension

I now come to give you three practical deductions.

First, is Christ's body now in heaven? Then I infer, O you that can lay a well-grounded claim for an interest in Jesus Christ: O, be not afraid to die, because your Christ is in heaven, and when you die, death is but a trapdoor to let you into endless joy where Christ is. Why, should we be as children to look on death as a bugbear, but look upon death as being a passage to your Father's house, as being a trapdoor to let you in where Jesus Christ is, Genesis 45:25, 27: "And they went up out of Egypt, and came into the land of Canaan unto Jacob their father…. And they told him all the words of Joseph, which he had said unto them: and when he saw the wagons which Joseph had sent to carry him, the spirit of Jacob their father revived." Did Jacob rejoice to see a wagon or a chariot that would carry him to Egypt to see his son Joseph, and will not you rejoice to think that death is a chariot to carry you to Jesus Christ, to carry you to heaven? O therefore let not your heart be troubled to die, because death is but a chariot to carry you to heaven! Is Christ gone into heaven?

Then, secondly, labor while you live on the earth to ascend to Christ in divine and holy ejaculations and meditations. Is Christ in heaven? Then why should not your heart be where your head is; why should you be groveling on the earth, seeing your Christ is now in heaven? It is a speech of Christ, Song of Solomon 3:6: "Who is this that cometh out of the wilderness like pillars of smoke, perfumed with myrrh and frankincense, with all powders of the merchant?" You should ascend up to Christ, though you are in trouble in the wilderness of this world. O ascend up to Christ in holy meditations; this use the apostle makes of it, Colossians 3:1: "If ye then be risen with Christ, seek those things which are above, where Christ sitteth on the right hand of God." The argument is, where Christ sits at the right hand of God, set your affections there. And so in Philippians 3:20: "For our conversation is in heaven; from whence also we look for the Saviour, the Lord Jesus Christ." Christ is in heaven; therefore, our conversation must be where our head is. It is a notable text, Matthew 24:28: "For wheresoever the carcass is, there will the eagles be gathered together." That Christ is in heaven it should make you ascend in your hearts heavenward. It is true, there are some that wrest these words, and give this sense of them, that they make the carcass to be the Jews and the eagles to be the Romans, because the Romans did use the eagle in their banner and ensign of war. Therefore, they say where the Jews were, the Romans should come. Though this was a truth, yet not the scope of the text, it is generally overthrown by most interpreters; but Gerrard chiefly refers these words to the day of judgment, where the carcass is thither will the eagles resort, that is, where Jesus Christ is in heaven, as the eagles do follow after the carcass to feed upon that, so the people of God shall be gathered about Jesus Christ, and this I do confess is the chief scope of the place, and do believe it is the chief intention of the Holy Ghost. But Gerrard makes another use of it too and refers it to the power and efficacy of the gospel in this life; Christ is now in heaven, says Gerrard, and the gospel shall be so powerful on men in the world that it shall make men as eager to come after Christ into heaven as the eagle is after the prey.

Thirdly, I infer hence that before you presume to apply the benefits and the comforts of Christ's ascension into heaven, labor to feel in your own hearts the efficacy of Christ's death and ascension. Every man applies the benefits of Christ's death and resurrection, and Christ's ascension before they find the efficacy of His death and the efficacy of His resurrection. It is the apostle's word, says he, "I labor to find the power of His resurrection"; so do you labor to find the power of His death, and the power of His ascension, before you find the comfort of it. It is to make you less earthly-minded, more passionately eager, and importunately earnest after the Lord Jesus Christ. Do you feel the power of the ascension to make you more heavenly minded, and less earthly-minded? O labor to feel the efficacy and power of it, else I might say to you as Jacob said to his mother in Genesis 27:12, "My father peradventure will feel me, and I shall seem to him as a deceiver, and I shall bring a curse and not a blessing." Nay, without peradventure God will feel and try whether you are the men or no that have right to the blessing, that shall have any real advantage and benefit by Christ's death, by Christ's ascension. God will try whether you do not seek to deceive your souls and deceive God Himself. If so, you will rather have a curse than a blessing, if you seek to apply the comfort of Christ's ascension before you feel the efficacy of it on your own hearts.

The Manner of Christ's Ascension

How did Christ ascend? First, Christ went to heaven visibly, in Acts 1. It was no transient glance of the eye, but they steadfastly beheld Jesus Christ; they saw Him when He went away. Again, secondly, Christ went to heaven bodily; therefore, those do err that hold that only His soul did go to heaven, and His body perished as others do. Thirdly, He went to heaven locally; He ascended locally. There are some men who hold that every place is heaven where God is. That is a truth, but heaven is a distinct place from the earth and hell. Christ had a mutation of place from the earth to the third heaven. Therefore, says He, the earth shall hold Me no more. Fourthly, He did ascend into heaven powerfully. Indeed, other men went to heaven bodily, not by their own strength, but it was by a borrowed strength. Elias had a fiery chariot to carry him to heaven, but Christ had none, for He went to heaven by His own strength. Lastly, Christ went to heaven eminently and singly. There are three bodies in heaven: there is the body of Enoch, the body of Elias, and the body of Christ. All else in heaven are saints and angels. Enoch went to heaven bodily as a type of Christ's ascension before the law, and Elias under the law and Christ under the gospel. Divines say that this shows there was salvation by Christ before the law, and salvation by Christ under the law, and salvation by Christ in the time of the gospel, but there is a difference between their going to heaven:

1. Enoch and Elijah went to heaven but they did not die and rise from the dead and then ascend into heaven. But first

Christ died, and then Christ was raised out of the grave, and then within forty days He ascended into heaven. There was one difference. Again, they did not ascend to heaven by their own strength, but by the power of God, they ascended into heaven. But we have got no good by their ascension, no benefit, nor merit accrues unto us by their being in heaven, but there is great benefit redounding to us by Christ's being in heaven. For, says Christ, "I go to heaven to prepare a place for you."

2. Enoch went to heaven, but he could not give the Spirit; so Elijah went to heaven, but he could not give the Spirit. Yes, but our Lord Jesus Christ, He is gone bodily into heaven. He has ascended up on high, and has given gifts unto men.

3. They went to heaven, said Polanus,[4] only as citizens of heaven. But Christ went to heaven as the Lord of heaven, who is there in His body and in His person, and these are the short and transient hints that I have given you on the first part of my text.

---

4. Amandus Polanus (1561–1610), German Reformed orthodox theologian, student of Beza, Professor of Old Testament at Basel, and author of numerous influential works, such as his *Syntagma theologiae Christianae* (1609–1610).

CHAPTER 3

Christ's Preparations for His People

I come now to the second thing in the text, to the benefit that believers have by Christ's going bodily into heaven: "I go to prepare a place for you." The observation is this: the fruit and benefit that all the elect of God have by Christ's going into heaven is to prepare a place for them there, "I go to prepare a place for you." Now in the handling of this doctrine there are three particulars.

First, I shall show you in what sense Christ's going bodily into heaven prepares heaven for believers. Secondly, I shall show you how can this Scripture say that by Christ's ascension heaven was prepared for us, when other Scriptures say that heaven was prepared for us from the beginning of the world. Thirdly, whether the patriarchs and righteous holy men of God that lived before Christ's ascension did go into heaven. Whither went they when they died? Therefore, the Church of Rome gathers from this text that before Christ went to heaven there was none [that] went to heaven, but all went into a place called *Limbus Patrum*.[1]

---

1. Also known as "Abraham's Bosom," in Roman Catholic theology, the *Limbus Patrum* was the place where the saints in the Old Testament were confined until they were freed by Christ in His "descent into hell."

Preparations Made by Christ's Ascension

First, in what sense may it be said that Christ by His going into heaven prepares a place for believers there? I answer in these three regards Christ by going into heaven prepares a place there.

1. By way of representation, Christ is not gone to heaven as other men, as a single and private person; but Christ is gone into heaven as a common and public person. Christ is gone up to heaven with flesh and blood, and with our natures He is gone to heaven; He is gone there as a representer of all the elect. Jesus Christ is gone to heaven representing the persons of the elect of God upon the earth. Hence it is that you have a passage, Ephesians 2:6, "And hath raised us up together, and made us sit together in heavenly places in Christ Jesus." We are not in heavenly places—we are in earthly places—but we do sit in heaven; because Christ is now in heaven, He is gone to heaven as a common and public person, a representer of all the elect, Hebrews 6:20, "Whither the forerunner is for us entered, even Jesus, made an high priest for ever after the order of Melchisedec." He did not go there for Himself but for us. Christ died as a public person representing all the elect of God, and Christ did go to heaven as a public person and has taken possession of heaven in our stead; Christ keeps our inheritance there, says Grotius, Christ is said to prepare a place for us in heaven. As a company of travelers, when they are going on a journey; they send one man before them to be their harbinger, to take up lodging in the inn and make provision for them when they come to the inn; our Lord Jesus Christ is gone to heaven before to prepare a place for the elect there.

2. Christ prepares a place for the elect by way of intercession. Hebrews 9:24: "For Christ is not entered into the holy places made with hands, which are the figures of the true; but into heaven itself, now to appear in the presence of God for us." That as the priest under the law, when he went to the holy places, he

had the names of all the tribes on his breast, so the Lord Jesus Christ, our great high priest, having the names of all the elect not only on His breast but in His heart, prayed to His Father that we might come there, and this intercession is another way that heaven is prepared for the elect.

3. Christ is said to prepare heaven for us by way of operation in us. He prepares heaven for us by preparing us for heaven, and this is the sense that Augustine[2] gives of these words. Jesus Christ prepares a mansion for us in heaven when He prepares us [to be] the inhabitants for heaven. Here is the great evidence for heaven: are your hearts prepared? Then you may be assured that heaven is prepared for you. Colossians 1:12–14: "Giving thanks unto the Father, which hath made us meet to be partakers of the inheritance of the saints in light: Who hath delivered us from the power of darkness, and hath translated us into the kingdom of his dear Son: In whom we have redemption through his blood, even the forgiveness of sins." An unconverted man is not a meet man for heaven. Now when Christ makes you meet for heaven, He then prepares a place for you. First Peter 1:3–5: "Blessed be the God and Father of our Lord Jesus Christ, which according to his abundant mercy hath begotten us again unto a lively hope by the resurrection of Jesus from the dead, To an inheritance incorruptible, and undefiled, and that fadeth not away, reserved in heaven for you, Who are kept by the power of God through faith unto salvation ready to be revealed in the last time." So that, beloved, if you are kept for heaven, and made meet for heaven, that is a demonstration that heaven is prepared for you.

---

2. Augustine of Hippo (354–430), church father and bishop, whose *Confessions* and works on biblical exegesis helped to lay the foundation for medieval and modern Christian thought.

Heaven Manifested by Christ's Ascension

I come now to the second query, which is this: how can the Scripture say that by Christ's ascension heaven is prepared for us when other Scriptures say that heaven was prepared for us from the beginning of the world? Matthew 25:34: "Then shall the King say unto them on his right hand, Come, ye blessed of my Father, inherit the kingdom prepared for you from the foundation of the world." Now if a kingdom was prepared for them from the beginning of the world, how does this Scripture appropriate a preparing of the kingdom of heaven only from the ascension of Christ? Divines do answer that you must distinguish between the decrees of God, and the clear manifestation and full execution of those decrees. Now if you respect the decrees of God, then the Scripture is true that the kingdom of heaven is prepared from the beginning of the world, for the decree and purpose of God was, before the world was, that the elect should have heaven as an inheritance; but if you expect the clear manifestation of it, then it was not till Jesus Christ ascended, and the distinction this Scripture allows of, especially in the point of justification, in this point the Scripture clears this distinction, Hebrews 9:8, "The Holy Ghost this signifying, that the way into the holiest of all was not yet made manifest, while as the first tabernacle was yet standing." The meaning is this: that the way to heaven was not manifest to the Jews while their tabernacle stood; that is, while their Levitical ceremonies were in use, the way to heaven was not manifest; the godly went to heaven before Christ's time, but it was not manifested, for the common sort of the Jews did not understand that by Jesus Christ's passion and ascension they must come to heaven; therefore, the apostle says, the way to the holiest of all was not yet manifested while their first tabernacle stood. So my text is true that heaven was prepared for believers by the Lord Jesus Christ's ascension.

Old Testament Saints Prepared by Christ

The third query is this: but you will say, if Christ by His ascension into heaven did prepare heaven for believers, then what became of all the people of God and holy men of God under the Old Testament? Whither went they?

The Jesuits raise the difficulty from the text. They say that before Christ ascended none did go to heaven; therefore, they make Abraham, Isaac, and Jacob, with all the patriarchs and all the holy men of God, to be in the place called *Limbus Patrum*, which was for the good men till Christ's ascension. Then there is *Limbus Infantum*,[3] a place of receipt of infants. Then there is *Purgatory*,[4] for men guilty of gross sins; heaven and hell they concur in to be a truth. *Limbus Patrum*, say they, was the place to receive all the good men till Christ's ascension, and then Christ took them all into heaven. Protestant divines take a deal of pains to vindicate this text.

If you will ask me what is become of the patriarchs and all good men of old before Christ's going into heaven, how can they come to heaven if heaven be prepared by Christ's ascension?

1. I may say that of Christ's ascension as Gerrard does of Christ's passion: the death of Christ was available before it was in being, so I may say of Christ's ascension, that it was available before it was in being. Gerrard has another passage, that the benefits we have by Christ are not only to be restrained to ages that are to come after Christ but to look backward to all ages before Christ.[5] Revelation 5:9: "And they sung a new

---

3. The "children's limbo"; in Roman Catholic theology, it is the place where infants who died before baptism were thought to have gone.

4. In medieval and Roman Catholic belief, the place of purification in which the souls of those who die in a state of grace undergo the process of purification before entering heaven.

5. *Margin:* "Beneficia Christi valent non solum antrorsum sed retrorsum. *Ger. loc. com.*" The citation can be found in John Gerhard, *Loci Theologici* (Berlin, 1870), 8:120.

song, saying, Thou art worthy to take the book, and to open the seals thereof: for thou wast slain, and hast redeemed us to God by thy blood out of every kindred, and tongue, and people, and nation." Not only was the Lamb slain decretively in God's decree, nor only is the Lamb slain typically in the ceremonial sacrifices but also virtually; there was virtue in Jesus Christ that all the godly Jews had virtue by Christ's death. There is my first answer.

2. Observe this: that the Scripture does not say that Christ by going up to heaven did open heaven for us; He being our Mediator sitting at God's right hand in heaven, heaven was opened before but not so fully adorned as it was by Christ's ascension, Hebrews 9:8, "The Holy Ghost this signifying, that the way into the holiest of all was not yet made manifest, while as the first tabernacle was yet standing." The Grecians do observe that Christ does not use a word that signifies to open a thing that is shut but to open, clear, and manifest a thing that is obscure; it was open before.

3. Against the Jesuits' conceit of *Limbus Patrum* there are clear passages in the Scripture, and undeniable reasons drawn from the Scripture that prove believers under the Old Testament went to heaven before Christ's ascension, as in Luke 16:22: "And it came to pass, that the beggar died, and was carried by the angels into Abraham's bosom: the rich man also died, and was buried." He lived two thousand years and more before Christ was born. Heaven is called Abraham's bosom, and the elect that died are said to go into Abraham's bosom, and Elijah and Enoch are in heaven, Hebrews 11:5: "By faith Enoch was translated that he should not see death; and was not found, because God had translated him." Verse 16: "But now they desire a better country, that is, an heavenly: wherefore God is not ashamed to be called their God: for he hath prepared for them a city." He is not ashamed to be their God; therefore, they have a city prepared

for them by God that likewise Lazarus was said to be carried by angels into Abraham's bosom; this was before Christ died. Then frequent Scriptures there are touching Christ's transfiguration, that when Christ was taken up, that He saw Moses and Elias; from thence divines gather that they must be in heaven.

There are four undeniable reasons [that] will prove that the godly before Christ's ascension went to heaven.

1. It appears by this because it is said that those that were carried to heaven were carried to heaven by the angels; the angels carried Lazarus into Abraham's bosom. Now certainly angels are not in *Limbus Patrum*, Luke 16:22.

2. Again, if the believers of old should not go into heaven, the death and merits of Christ would be extenuated, Hebrews 13:8: "Jesus Christ the same yesterday, and to day, and for ever." He was the same yesterday, that is, before He was born, He was of use then, as well as to after time.

3. Again, if the souls of wicked men be in hell before Christ's time, then the souls of godly men must be in heaven before Christ's time. That must clearly follow by the rule of contraries. Now that wicked men went to hell is clear, Jude 7: "Even as Sodom and Gomorrha, and the cities about them in like manner, giving themselves over to fornication, and going after strange flesh, are set forth for an example, suffering the vengeance of eternal fire." They went to hell before Christ's time; therefore, it must follow clearly that the elect must go to heaven before Christ's time.

4. There is the very same reason why believers should go to heaven before Christ's ascension, as there is why they should go to heaven after Christ's ascension: because believers under the Old Testament had the same gospel preached to them as now we have, and they had the same Spirit, the same faith, and under the same covenant, and therefore why must not they go to the same place? I shall clearly prove this unto you. First, they had the same

Spirit and the same faith that we have, and this is laid down by the apostle, in 2 Corinthians 4:13, "We having the same spirit of faith, according as it is written, I believed, and therefore have I spoken; we also believe, and therefore speak." And they with us had the same justifying faith. Their circumcision was a sign of righteousness by faith. And then again, they had the same gospel that we have, Hebrews 4:2, "For unto us was the gospel preached, as well as unto them: but the word preached did not profit them, not being mixed with faith in them that heard it." The same gospel, only theirs is dark, for the ceremonial law was gospel, merely types and shadows of Christ to come, shadows of salvation by Christ's blood. Nay, they had the same Christ as we have, 1 Corinthians 10:4: "And did all drink the same spiritual drink: for they drank of that spiritual Rock that followed them: and that Rock was Christ." And in the wilderness it is said, let not us tempt Christ as they also tempted Him. They sinned against Christ in the wilderness, and they enjoyed Christ in the wilderness. So that they had the same Christ as we have. Again, they are under the same covenant that we are, Jeremiah 31. It is the same covenant with ours in Hebrews 8. Is there not then the same reason why believers under the Old Testament should go to the same place as believers under the New? For they had the same Spirit, the same faith, the same gospel, the same Christ, and [are] under the same covenant; therefore, they must go to the same place, though heaven is prepared by Christ's ascension, yet heaven was open before, yet not so manifested before since Christ died, rose, and went up to heaven.

Practical Inferences from Christ's Preparations

I now come to draw out a few practical inferences from this doctrine, which are four. If it be so that Jesus Christ, by His going to heaven has prepared a place for the elect there, then learn by way of recompense, by way of compensation, and by way of gratification to Jesus Christ. O prepare a heart for Christ who has prepared a heaven for you! Shall Christ go to heaven to prepare a place for you, and will you afford Christ no corner in your heart? You let your lusts sit on the throne of your heart, yet you do not give Christ any room there. We read in Revelation 19:7: "Let us be glad and rejoice, and give honour to him: for the marriage of the Lamb is come, and his wife hath made herself ready." O, be as the bride: make yourself ready for the marriage day. The betrothing day was when Christ went up to heaven; your marriage day is your dying day. O against the marriage day of the Lamb, do you who are His bride make yourself ready; do you prepare a heart for Christ, who has prepared heaven for you. Origen[6] has a good passage on Luke 22:12, "And he shall shew you a large upper room furnished: there make ready," though he does much abuse the scope of the Scripture. There were three properties of the room wherein Christ ate the Passover: a large, upper, and a furnished room. He makes this allegory of it: "I do not give it to you as the sense of it, but take his gloss, that if you will come to sup with Christ, you must make your heart as the upper room, a heart raised in divine contemplation; and not only an upper room but a large room, a large heart, a furnished room, a heart adorned with grace. O, do prepare a large room, an upper room, and a furnished room for Christ!

Secondly, if Christ be gone into heaven to prepare a place for the elect, then we are rather gainers than losers by the want of Christ's bodily presence. We should be less happy to have Christ upon the earth than now Christ is in heaven, for we are greater gainers by Christ's now being in heaven than if He were with us in person upon the earth. Divines illustrate this: say they, the

---

6. Origen (ca. 185–ca. 254), the most influential biblical scholar and theologian of the early Greek church; he made copious use of the allegorical method and believed that Scripture had multiple senses or meanings.

body of the sun is sixth in the firmament and gives light over all the world; now should the body of the sun be taken from the firmament and be upon the earth amongst us, it would not be of that avail to us as now it is. The Son of Righteousness now [that] He is in the heavens, He is of greater avail to us than if He were upon the earth; for if He were on the earth, all the world could not see Him at once, so that we are greater gainers by Christ's gong up to heaven than if He were in person here amongst us, as God says in John 14:28, "Ye have heard how I said unto you, I go away, and come again unto you. If ye loved me, ye would rejoice, because I said, I go unto the Father: for my Father is greater than I." Truly, it was matter of joy and not of grief that Christ left this world and went to heaven, because He went there to prepare a place for us. I would fain know whether Jacob would have been troubled for his son Joseph, if Jacob had known this, that his son was gone into Egypt to prepare a place for him and all his brethren, against the famine; surely it would never have troubled him. Truly your Joseph, your Jesus, has gone to heaven to prepare a place for you there. Therefore, let it not trouble you, seeing you are more happy by Christ's presence in heaven than if you had His bodily presence upon the earth.

Thirdly, if Christ be gone bodily into heaven, it is a ground of comfort to you that though you have no place to put your head here in this world, yet remember Christ is gone to prepare heaven for you. It may be many of you have poor cottages, smoky houses. Why, for all that, lift up your heart with joy that Christ has gone to prepare a large palace in heaven for you. When Valens,[7] the Arian emperor, threatened Basil,[8] and said that neither by sea nor land would be safe from his power, yet, says

---

7. Flavius Valens (328–378), Roman emperor baptized by the Arian bishop of Constantinople; he sought to minimize theological conflicts in the early church but sided with the Arian faction.

8. Basil of Caesarea (329–379), an early church father who defended the

Basil, "For all the emperor's rage, I shall be either in heaven or under heaven." Why so, though you may be driven to and fro, by sea and land, and have no abiding place of safety to put your head in, yet in spite of the malice of men and devils, you shall be either in heaven or under heaven. A cardinal threatened Luther[9] with this, that there should not be a place left for Luther in all the empire. "O," says Luther, smilingly, "if earth cannot keep me, yet heaven shall." Beloved, bear up your hearts; though you may not have an abiding place on earth, yet you have one prepared for you in heaven.

Fourthly, is Christ gone into heaven to prepare a place for believers? Then all Christless and graceless men have no benefit by the passion or ascension of our Lord Jesus Christ. Christ died but not for you. Christ rose again, but not for you. Christ is gone up to heaven but not for you. He will prepare no place in heaven for you. Therefore, your case is, as was spoken of Judas, Acts 1:25: "That he may take part of this ministry and apostleship, from which Judas by transgression fell, that he might go to his own place." It was to no place of Christ's preparing; it was to a place prepared of old for condemnation. In the phrase of Jude, "Tophet is prepared of old." It is a place prepared of an angry God, and not a place prepared by a Mediator. This therefore should be matter of astonishment to all Christless and graceless men. What though Christ be gone into heaven? Yet you shall never follow after Him. What though Christ prepares a place for all His elect? Yet He prepares none for you. Your place is prepared by an angry God. You go to hell, and not to a place prepared by Jesus Christ.

---

orthodox faith against the Arians; he also wrote influential works on the Holy Spirit and the monastic life.

9. Martin Luther (1483–1546), German professor of theology and pioneer of the Protestant Reformation.

And thus I have done with the second doctrine, to wit, that the fruit and benefit that all the elect of God have by Christ's going into heaven, it is to prepare a place for them. "I go to prepare a place for you."

CHAPTER 4

The Comfort of Christ's Second Coming

The third main doctrine is the doctrine of Christ's coming again: "I go and prepare a place for you, but I will come again." Christ may stay long, but He will not stay forever. But the Christ who said He would go away also said He would come again. To explicate the phrase, "I will come again," what is meant by Christ's coming again? Beloved, there are four sorts of interpretations of these words, none of which are true but the last.

First, by "coming again," some understand Christ's first coming. So the Jews understand it (for some of them study the Evangelists; though they study to confute it, they do not believe that Christ is come); they make it of His coming in the flesh. [In] John 4, it was the woman's sense of the coming of Christ in the 25th verse: "The woman saith unto him, I know that Messias cometh, which is called Christ: when he is come, he will tell us all things." Why, He was come, but she thought that He had not been come. "O," says Jesus Christ, "I am He. I am come already!" So the Jews and the Samaritans ever took the phrase of Christ's coming not to judge the world but of the coming in the flesh.

Secondly, it cannot be understood of the coming of Christ by His Spirit. So some interpreters do understand the words, "but I will come again, by my Spirit," and they make it agreeable to that phrase, "Lo, I go away, but I will be with you to the end of the world." But Calvin rejects it because the next words say, "I will come again, to receive you to myself."

Thirdly, it cannot be meant, as the Millenaries[1] understand it, of Christ's coming again to remain a thousand years upon the earth; and for that I shall give you several demonstrations from Scripture when I come to handle it.

Fourthly, by Christ's coming again it is to be understood, as Calvin and most interpreters take it, Christ's coming to judge the world, as if He should say, "I go to prepare heaven for you, and I promise you to come again, that though your bodies die and rot in the graves, yet I will come again and raise you up another day, and receive you unto Myself." It is to be understood of His last coming. And thus much for the explication of the phrase.

The Comfort of Christ's Return

Christ here gives His followers a promise of His coming to comfort their troubled hearts. From thence observe that Christ's coming again to judge the world is a doctrine full of comfort to every believer while they are here upon the earth. For the proof of this, see 1 Thessalonians 4:15 to the end, "For this we say unto you by the word of the Lord, that we which are alive and remain unto the coming of the Lord shall not prevent them which are asleep. For the Lord himself shall descend from heaven with a shout, with the voice of the archangel, and with the trump of God: and the dead in Christ shall rise first: Then we which are alive and remain shall be caught up together with them in the clouds, to meet the Lord in the air: and so shall we ever be with the Lord. Wherefore comfort one another with these words." In the handling of this there are four queries to be answered:

---

1. Those who believe in a literal thousand-year reign of Christ upon earth.

Patience Pays Off

The first is by way of objection. What comfort is it to us that Christ should bid them they should not be troubled, that He might come again, when between the making of this promise and this time promised it has run above 1600 years already? I answer:

1. That tract of time can neither interrupt the accomplishment of a promise, nor the comfort of a promise; it is comfortable that what is promised shall sooner or later come to pass, Daniel 10:1, "In the third year of Cyrus king of Persia a thing was revealed unto Daniel, whose name was called Belteshazzar; and the thing was true, but the time appointed was long: and he understood the thing, and had understanding of the vision." It is a promise made by Christ to comfort you against all the troubles of the world. He will come again, and though the time be long ere He comes, yet the time appointed will be true. It is certain, though it be long.

2. The godly in ages before us could rejoice in promises made to them, though the accomplishment thereof was not fulfilled till many years after. And why should not the disciples do so then? And why should not we do so now? I will give you two or three instances: John 8:56: "Your Father Abraham rejoiced to see my day: and he saw it, and was glad." The promise was made to Abraham above a thousand years before he saw Him, and yet he was glad. Hebrews 11:13: "These all died in faith, not having received the promises, but having seen them afar off, and were persuaded of them, and embraced them." They did embrace the promises, though they were far off in their accomplishment. An excellent text you have in Isaiah 9:6: "For unto us a child is born, unto us a son is given: and the government shall be upon his shoulders," &c. Behold, this is [a] matter of joy: "For to us a child is born, and unto us a son is given." They might have said, "Lord what is that to us? We hear of garments rolled in blood, and of the confused noise of warriors, and dost Thou tell us of that

which shall not be till many years after?" And yet the prophet thinks no fitter a promise to give them than the promise that a virgin should conceive a son. I mention it for this, that though promises were made long since, yet bear up your hearts for that it will be sure and certain though it be long. And so much for the first particular.

Proof of Comfort

The next particular is, yes, but how does it appear that Christ's coming to judge the world is a doctrine so full of comfort to believers?

1. It appears by the believers' longing and looking for Christ's coming to judge the world. It is the property of God's people to long for the appearance of Christ. When it makes the heart of a Felix to tremble, it is a doctrine of great comfort to a believer. It is called "the day of redemption," and called by Peter "the day of refreshing." And this made the church say, "Come, Lord Jesus, come quickly." This shows that to the people of God there is no doctrine so comfortable as the doctrine of Christ's coming to judge the world, Titus 2:13: "Looking for that blessed hope, and the glorious appearing of the great God and our Saviour Jesus Christ." Second Peter 3:12: "Looking for and hasting unto the coming of the day of God, wherein the heavens being on fire shall be dissolved, and the elements shall melt with fervent heat"; 2 Timothy 4:8: "Henceforth there is laid up for me a crown of righteousness, which the Lord, the righteous judge, shall give me at that day: and not to me only, but unto all them also that love his appearing." A crown is laid up for me, and not for me only, but for all them that love his appearing. This shows that surely it must be a doctrine of great comfort to the elect of God, because they so long and look for, and love the coming of Jesus Christ.

2. It is a doctrine of great comfort because Jesus Christ has reserved the full glorification of the elect for that time. Though Christ brings souls to heaven before His coming, yet He does not completely glorify any of His servants till His coming again to judge the world, 1 John 3:2: "Beloved, now are we the sons of God, and it doth not yet appear what we shall be: but we know that, when he shall appear, we shall be like him; for we shall see him as he is." And in Colossians 3:4: "When Christ, who is our life, shall appear, then shall ye also appear with him in glory." God has reserved the full glorification of the elect until the time of His coming, 1 Peter 5:4: "And when the chief Shepherd shall appear, ye shall receive a crown of glory that fadeth not away." Frequent texts of Scripture there are to prove the reserve that Christ has of the full glorifying of the elect. It is at the time of His coming to judge the world.

Special Situations of Comfort

The third particular is: but wherein is the doctrine of Christ's coming again so comfortable to believers? There are these four particulars more especially wherein the doctrine of Christ's coming again to judge the world is a doctrine full of comfort to believers.

1. In case of any scandalous aspersion, or any unjust imputation that is laid upon them, it may serve for great comfort to you in this case. The apostle gives it to you in 1 Corinthians 4:3–4: "But with me it is a very small thing that I should be judged of you, or of man's judgment: yea, I judge not mine own self. For I know nothing by myself; yet am I not hereby justified: but he that judgeth me is the Lord." Censure me what you will, and judge of me what you please, for He that judges me shall be the Lord; therefore, it is a small matter that I am judged of you.

Suppose you are judged, you are scandalized, and you are aspersed in the world; appeal to Jesus Christ in heaven, for He that judges you is the Lord. And this we find Christ did in 1 Peter 2:23: "Who, when he was reviled, reviled not again; when he suffered, he threatened not; but committed himself to him that judgeth righteously." When you are reviled, and aspersed, and censured, do not revile again; do not censure again, but do as Christ did. Commit your cause to Christ who judges all things righteously. Christ will come to over-judge all things that have been judged amiss, Jude15: "To execute judgment upon all, and to convince all that are ungodly among them of all their ungodly deeds which they have ungodly committed, and of all their hard speeches which ungodly sinners have spoken against him." Men have hard speeches against many who are upright in the land; it is a comfort, then, that of Christ's coming again, one end is to convince men of all their hard speeches and scandalous aspersions.

2. Christ's coming again is a doctrine of comfort in case of all persecution you undergo from men, for Christ, for the gospel, 2 Thessalonians 1:6–7: "Seeing it is a righteous thing with God to recompense tribulation to them that trouble you; And to you who are troubled rest with us, when the Lord Jesus shall be revealed from heaven with his mighty angels." [It is] as if He should have said, "You are troubled and persecuted about the gospel, for Christ's sake. Why, be not troubled, for Christ is coming from heaven." First Peter 4:13: "But rejoice, inasmuch as ye are partakers of Christ's sufferings; that, when his glory shall be revealed, ye may be glad also with exceeding joy." When Christ comes to be revealed and to judge the world, you shall be glad also with exceeding joy; that is a second case wherein this doctrine may be of comfort.

3. This doctrine may serve for comfort in case of any inward accusation of conscience from the apprehension of your own guiltiness. It may be you judge yourself that you are a damned, undone creature. Remember that there is a judgment to pass

on you besides your own mistake and misapprehension. Christ's coming to judgment should be a comfort to you against your own inward accusation, because He that is your Jesus is your Judge. He is your Advocate to plead your cause, and your Judge to judge your cause. Suppose your conscience accuses you, and you judge yourself to hell, yet comfort yourself with this: that your Jesus will afterwards come to judge you.

4. Christ's coming again to judge the world is a doctrine of comfort in case of oppression in courts of judicature. What though might overcomes right, and the usurping hand uses ways of oppression and violence towards you? It matters not. For Christ's coming to judgment shall be of great comfort to you. Jerome[2] says that Christ shall come to judge things that are not judged in the world, and Christ shall come to judge things that are judged amiss in the world. Christ shall judge all oppression and violence that is done by a usurping hand. Here is matter of comfort, that Christ comes to judge them all over again. An excellent passage which Solomon has is Ecclesiastes 3:16–17: "And moreover I saw under the sun the place of judgment, that wickedness was there; and the place of righteousness, that iniquity was there. I said in mine heart, God shall judge the righteous and the wicked: for there is a time there for every purpose and for every work." That is, I saw into courts of judicature, and I saw wickedness was there; and I looked into the place of righteousness, and behold iniquity was there. Then I said in my heart, "Surely God shall judge both the righteous and the wicked." If there were no argument in all the Scripture to prove Christ's coming again, this argument will evince that Christ shall come to judge the world. There must be a judging

---

2. Jerome (ca. 347–419/20), biblical translator and Latin church father, whose works profoundly influenced the early Middle Ages; he is known particularly for his Latin translation of the Bible, the Vulgate.

over again. There shall be a general judgment because there is so much perverting of judgment here below. And thus you have wherein, or in what cases, the doctrine of Christ's coming may serve for comfort.

Recipients of Comfort
Fourthly, to whom will Christ's coming be a comfort?

1. To all tempted and troubled by Satan: this is the time of accomplishing that promise. Romans 16:20: "The God of peace shall bruise Satan under your feet shortly."

2. To all persecuted and opposed by men, 2 Thessalonians 1:6–7: "Seeing it is a righteous thing with God to recompense tribulation to them that trouble you; And to you who are troubled rest with us." [That is,] when the Lord Jesus shall be revealed from heaven with His mighty angels.

3. To all merciful ones, Matthew 25:34–36: "Then shall the King say unto them on his right hand, Come, ye blessed of my Father, inherit the kingdom prepared for you from the foundation of the world: For I was an hungered, and ye gave me meat: I was thirsty, and ye gave me drink: I was a stranger, and ye took me in." Second Timothy 1:16, 18: "The Lord give mercy unto the house of Onesiphorus; for he oft refreshed me, and was not ashamed of my chain.… The Lord grant unto him that he may find mercy of the Lord in that day."

4. To all who can lay a grounded claim of interest in Jesus Christ: His coming again will be comfortable then, 1 John 2:28: "And now, little children, abide in him; that, when he shall appear, we may have confidence, and not be ashamed before him at his coming."

5. Christ's coming again will be comfortable to all that judge themselves, 1 Corinthians 11:31: "For if we would judge ourselves, we should not be judged."

6. To all them that watch and pray, Luke 21:36: "Watch ye therefore, and pray always, that ye may be counted worthy to escape all these things that shall come to pass, and to stand before the Son of man."

7. To all believers it will be very comfortable, 1 Peter 1:7: "That the trial of your faith, being much more precious than of gold that perisheth, though it be tried with fire, might be found unto praise and honor and glory at the appearing of Jesus Christ."

Applications of Christ's Return

I now come to the application of the point, by way of caution. There are two cautions to be noted.

A Spur to Duty

First, though the doctrine of Christ's coming again be full of comfort yet take this caution: that you are to look on the doctrine of Christ's coming to judgment as a doctrine to teach you duty as well as to give you comfort. It is a great abuse of your privileges when you make any gospel point to be an inlet of comfort, and do not make that very comfort to be a spur to duties, and the Scripture puts you upon this, 1 Corinthians 1:7: "So that ye come behind in no gift; waiting for the coming of our Lord Jesus Christ." Second Thessalonians 2:1–2: "Now we beseech you, brethren, by the coming of our Lord Jesus Christ… That ye be not soon shaken in mind." He presses them to duty on this doctrine by the coming of Jesus Christ.

Now to speak distinctly to the caution, there are [six] duties to which the doctrine of Christ's coming is serviceable unto:

1. The doctrine of Christ's coming should teach you the duty of patience under all your sufferings in the world, James 5:8: "Be ye also patient; stablish your hearts: for the coming of the Lord draweth nigh."

2. It should serve to be a spur to the improving of your gifts under ordinances, not only patient under afflictions, but it should provoke you to improve your gifts under ordinances, 1 Corinthians 1:7: "So that ye come behind in no gift; waiting for the coming of our Lord Jesus Christ." The waiting for the coming of our Lord Jesus Christ should provoke you to a holy improvement of growth under ordinances, for Christ will call you to an account of your hearing, Revelation 22:17: "And the Spirit and the bride say, Come. And let him that heareth say, Come." You that are an unfaithful hearer, an unprofitable hearer, you dare not say as the Spirit says, "Lord come, Lord come," but he that grows better by hearing, he will say, "Lord come, Lord come"; a notable text, Matthew 25:22–23, "He also that had received two talents came and said, Lord, thou deliveredst unto me two talents: behold, I have gained two other talents besides them. His lord said unto him, Well done, good and faithful servant; thou hast been faithful over a few things, I will make thee ruler over many things: enter thou into the joy of thy lord." This is Christ's language as divines interpret, that when He will come to judge the world, He will call you, "Well done, thou good and faithful servant, thou hast improved thy gifts well; thou hast improved thy talents well."

3. This doctrine should provoke you to be conscionable in your outward calling, whether religious, or whether civil. "I wish," says Augustine, "that when Christ shall come, He might find me either preaching or praying."[3] Labor then to be about your work when Christ comes, for Christ to come and find you in the stews, to find you working of wickedness, O, how unmeet are you for Christ's coming!

4. This doctrine should be a spur to you to moderate the use of lawful comforts. Philippians 4:5: "Let your moderation

---

3. *In the margin: Aut precantem aut predicantem.*

be known unto all men. The Lord is at hand." Luke 21:34: "And take heed to yourselves, lest at any time your hearts be overcharged with surfeiting, and drunkenness, and cares of this life, and so that day come upon you unawares." It was Christ's counsel to His apostles, 1 Peter 4:7: "But the end of all things is at hand: be ye therefore sober, and watch unto prayer."

5. It should provoke you to repentance. Acts 17:30–31: "And the times of this ignorance God winked at; but now commandeth all men every where to repent: Because he hath appointed a day, in the which he will judge the world in righteousness by that man whom he hath ordained." The doctrine of God's appointing the day for the man Christ to judge the world should be a spur to the grace of repentance, that now every man everywhere should repent. Christ's coming should be a spur to repentance.

6. Christ's coming should be a spur to provoke you to keep a good conscience towards God and man in your living here in this world. Acts 24:15–16: "And have hope toward God, which they themselves also allow, that there shall be a resurrection of the dead, both of the just and unjust. And herein do I exercise myself, to have always a conscience void of offence toward God, and toward men." The thoughts of Christ's coming to judge the quick and the dead should make you have thoughts to get a good conscience void of offence towards God and man, 2 Peter 3:11: "Seeing then that all these things shall be dissolved, what manner of persons ought ye to be in all holy conversation and godliness"? And thus much is for the first caution, that you are to look on the coming of Christ as a doctrine serviceable as well for duty as comfort.

Beware of Bold Conclusions
The second caution is this: take heed of peremptory conclusions about this dark and obscure doctrine of Christ's coming to judge

the world. There are many loose and lavish frolic wits who have bold and adventurous attempts touching the coming of the Lord in determining that which the Scripture determines not. It is not my intent to trouble you with niceties, but only to check the frolic and bold attempts of some who go about to determine that which the Scripture does no way reveal, to which end take heed of these things:

1. Take heed of determining the place from whence Christ should come. The papists are bold this way. They hold you in hand that Christ shall come from the east. Therefore, our churches, all of them, were built east and west, and upon the ground, that Christ would come from the east. The Scripture says that Christ shall come as lightning from the east, but that does not show the place from whence He comes. But Christ's coming as lightning notes the visibility of His coming, and the celerity of Christ's coming. Lightning is visible, and so shall Christ's coming be; all shall see Him as you see lightning. Now this bold attempt has been the foundation to many superstitious opinions. It is the reason for bowing and cringing towards the east. All rose merely from that ground of Christ's coming from the east. The Scripture only says that He shall come down from heaven, and the Lord shall come from heaven, but from what part of the heaven the Scripture does not speak.

2. Pass not bold conjectures in determining the place where Christ shall come to judge the world. Many men where the Scripture is silent do run into many strong conceits to determine that which the Scripture does not. Many books do determine the place where Christ shall come to judge the world, and that is the valley of Jehoshaphat. And there is one text which seems to carry it that way, which is in Joel 3:12: "Let the heathen be wakened, and come up to the valley of Jehoshaphat: for there will I sit to judge all the heathen round about." Here they do conjecture that Christ shall come to the valley of Jehoshaphat, and there

He shall judge all the world, and I shall, to show the vanity and wickedness of these, give these in five[4] demonstrations: (1) It is not spoken of God the Son but of God the Father, to be your Judge; therefore, it cannot have a reference to the last judgment, for Christ judges then. (2) Their judgment here only refers to the judging of the heathen round about. Now the general judgment is for the judging of the righteous and the unrighteous. (3) That it is impossible that the valley of Jehoshaphat should contain all the men that ever were, that are, and that shall be in the world to be judged; therefore, it is not profitable that this has reference to the last judgment. (4) The time that this judgment here is spoken of is limited by the prophet himself; for compare this verse with the second verse: "I will also gather all nations, and will bring them down into the valley of Jehoshaphat, and will plead with them there for my people and for my heritage Israel, whom they have scattered among the nations, and parted my land." The time is spoken of when God shall turn again the captivity of Judah and Jerusalem; then God should judge the Babylonians, and those heathen nations that assisted them for to undo the people of God; therefore, it refers to some time after the captivity, and not to the general and last coming of the Son of God. And so much for taking off that text from yielding patronage to that fond conceit of Christ's coming to judge the world in the valley of Jehoshaphat. The Scripture is far from giving you the place where Christ shall come to judgment, either in the valley of Jehoshaphat or mount Olivet but only in the air. First Thessalonians 4:17: "Then we which are alive and remain shall be caught up together with them in the clouds, to meet the Lord in the air: and so shall we ever be with the Lord." The Scripture makes no mention of Christ's coming upon the

---

4. Love only provides four demonstrations.

earth at all. Take heed of bold attempts and conjectures about the place of Christ's judgment.

3. Take heed of bold attempts about the time of Christ's judgment. There have been them which have shown an abundance of wickedness in this. Gerrard confutes the folly of such men who guess at the time when Christ shall come to judge the world. Augustine mentions that some in his time held that Christ should come to judge the world a thousand years after his death; but we have seen their folly and shame, for there is more time expired than that. Another says that some held in his time that Christ would come to judge the world 365 years after his death; that is a folly likewise, for there is more time passed than that. Luther says that there were Anabaptists who held that in the year 1530 Christ would come to judge the world, but we have seen their folly likewise, for there is more time passed than that. Napier,[5] though a learned nobleman in Scotland, was too frolic in this way, for he boldly says that Christ shall come to judge the world in the year 1688. But beloved, Christ's coming to judge the world cannot be determined, for Christ would not even gratify His own apostles to tell them the time when His coming would be, Matthew 24. He would not tell them when the end of the world should be. It shows then it is great pride of heart to pass peremptory conjectures upon the period of time. Christ did not think it meet to tell His apostles of the time of His coming, 1 Thessalonians 5:1: "But of the times and the seasons, brethren, ye have no need that I write unto you." Nay, angels in heaven, and Christ Himself, as He was mere man, could not tell the time, Mark 13:32: "But of that day and that hour knoweth no man, no, not the angels which are in

---

5. John Napier (1550–1617), nicknamed Marvellous Merchiston, was a Scottish landowner, mathematician, physicist, astronomer, and millenarian; though influential in multiple spheres of learning, he regarded his speculative work on the Book of Revelation as his greatest achievement.

heaven, neither the Son, but the Father." Matthew 24:36: "But of that day and hour knoweth no man, no, not the angels of heaven, but my Father only."

I only mention it for this, to show the vanity of our age, of those who will undertake to show the very day when Christ should come. Likewise, to condemn the former ages, who run to things not revealed. I remember what a learned man says, one that comments upon my text; says he, there is nothing that does expose the Christian religion to more contempt than the preachers and the hearers of it will run into nice questions and be peremptory in their resolves of that the Scripture speaks not of. And Jews and Gentiles may suspect the whole gospel, because they see men peremptory about things which are not revealed in the gospel and shall see their falsehood appearing to all. Be not peremptory in your determinations about the time of Christ's coming, nor about the place where, for neither is revealed in Scripture. Christ did deny His disciples when they asked Him where He should come. Luke 17:37: "And they answered and said unto him, Where, Lord? And he said unto them, Wheresoever the body is, tither will the eagles be gathered together." Christ told them of the destruction of Jerusalem and the end of the world. Then said the disciples, "But where, Lord, wilt Thou come?" Christ only gives them this answer, that where the carcass is, there will the eagles flee; that is, where Christ is, all the elect shall be gathered as birds of prey flock together after a carcass to feed upon. So that Christ would neither tell the place where, nor the time when; and this should be a check and a control to men's curious pryings about that which the Scripture is silent in.

Lastly, take heed of bold and adventurous conjectures about the manner of Christ's coming to judge the world, by vain and carnal corruptions and a temporal kingdom of Christ. Many are very peremptory about it, and there be strange books, at least in their own expressions, that they can descry the very manner of His coming, that Christ shall come from heaven and dwell a thousand years upon the earth, and the dead shall rise and live in the world. But these are such things which the Scripture never takes notice of.

CHAPTER 5

The Thousand-Year Reign of Christ

I am [now] to handle on this promise of Christ: "But I will come again." A perplexed query, which is this: whether Christ Jesus, in promising His disciples to come again, meant to come to reign upon the earth here a thousand years, or whether it be meant of Christ's last coming to judge the world. This Scripture and others are made use of and brought to prove that Christ shall come from heaven in person and live upon the earth for a whole thousand years. They fancy that Jesus Christ, when He shall come to this personal reign, shall raise all the martyrs who have lost their lives in His cause, and the devil shall be bound up so that he shall tempt men to sin no more, and wicked men shall be tied up that they shall not persecute the church of God. This is an ancient opinion, and almost since the apostles' days.

Before I give you my thoughts from the words touching Christ's coming, as they pretend, to reign a thousand years upon the earth, I shall show the rise of this opinion. First, from Eusebius[1] and others, they give us the rise of this opinion from Cerinthus,[2] which had it, who lived in the time of John. This

---

1. Eusebius of Caesarea (ca. 260–339), church historian and author of the first surviving history of the Christian church, *The Ecclesiastical History*, which has had a formative influence on Western culture.
2. Cerinthus (fl. 100), an early Gnostic heretic who held that the "Christ

Cerinthus, who was a pestilent heretic in those times, held that Christ was born by the conjunction of a man and woman, *Christum ex congressu maritali genitum esse*, and not born by a virgin, and was born as others are, and so must be a sinner. He was the man that was the first author from whom this opinion had any life or being. Eusebius says [that] Papias,[3] Bishop of Hieropolis, also held this opinion, not in so gross a way as Cerinthus did, but rather spiritually. And there was some spice of this in the apostles, for they did dream of a temporal kingdom; therefore, they asked Christ, when He was going to heaven, "Lord, when wilt Thou restore the kingdom unto Israel?" There was in the time of the apostles a fancy that Christ must be an earthly monarch, and destroy all the kings of the earth, and all the enemies of the world, and must come here to rule and reign a thousand years upon the earth. It was brought over into Germany and there [it] was taken hold by John of Leyden,[4] in Westphalia, and handed over to us in England by men of late. Now for the confutation.

Refuting the Millenarians

First, I shall quote express Scriptures that Christ shall not come in person out of heaven till His last coming to judge the world. Secondly, I shall give you some reasons from the Scripture as to why Christ cannot come out of heaven bodily and in person to reign a thousand years upon the earth. Thirdly, I shall show you some absurdities and incongruities that would follow if Christ should come to reign a thousand years upon the earth.

---

spirit" descended on Jesus at His baptism and left Him at the cross. Irenaeus reports the story that the apostle John refused to stay in the same bathhouse as Cerinthus, lest the roof fall down upon them.

3. Papias (ca. 60–ca. 130), bishop of Hieropolis, and apostolic father, whose works exist mainly in fragments. Tradition holds that Papias knew the apostle John and was a disciple of Polycarp. Later legend has it that he was John's amanuensis.

4. John of Leyden (1509–1536), a Dutch Anabaptist leader and millenarian; he proclaimed himself to be the King of New Jerusalem in 1534.

Scripture Says Christ Returns to Judge

First, for express Scriptures, which are four:

1. The first Scripture [is] Acts 3:21: "Whom the heaven must receive until the times of restitution of all things, which God hath spoken by the mouth of all his holy prophets since the world began." There the apostle tells you directly that the heaven must receive and keep Jesus Christ. How long? Till the restitution of all things. The Millenaries hold that the restitution of all things may be at the time of Christ's judging the world. First, there cannot be a total abolition of sin in the world, at the thousand years end. There shall be a number of men, and wicked, during the thousand years. All things cannot be restored, for sin brings the creature under a curse. It is apparent that it cannot be till Christ's last coming to judge the world, because other Scriptures tell you that the time of restitution cannot be till our bodies are raised from the dead, Romans 8:23: "And not only they, but ourselves also, which have the firstfruits of the Spirit, even we ourselves groan within ourselves, waiting for the adoption, to wit, the redemption of our body." That is, the creatures do, as it were, groan, being used by man as an instrument to God's dishonor, so that till the bodies of all the elect are redeemed and glorified, till that time the creature lies under a curse by reason of man's sins and man's abuse. And they themselves that plead for Christ's personal reign for a thousand years upon the earth, though they hold that the martyrs shall be raised at that time, yet do not hold that all the elect shall be raised at that time. Therefore, the apostle says expressly that the heavens must keep the person of Christ till the restitution of all things, till the bodies of the elect come to be raised from the dead. Again, it is apparent from the context in Acts 3 that the restitution of all things can intend no other time than the time of Christ's coming to judgment.

[Why so?] (1) Because it is said that the time here spoken of is when the Jews were to be refreshed from the Lord's presence.

Verses 19–21: "Repent ye therefore, and be converted, that your sins may be blotted out, when the times of refreshing shall come from the presence of the Lord. And he shall send Jesus Christ, which before was preached unto you: Whom the heaven must receive until the times of restitution of all things, which God hath spoken by the mouth of all his holy prophets since the world began." And they cannot be refreshed by the Lord's presence till Christ's coming to judgment and their resurrection. (2) It was the time that God solemnly declared pardon of sin for all the elect: "Repent ye therefore, and be converted, that your sins may be blotted out." (3) It is said, of which all the prophets bear witness, those that plead for Christ's personal reign of a thousand years upon the earth cannot say that all the prophets spoke this; for Moses, Daniel, and others, nay, none of the prophets speak of Christ's reign a thousand years upon earth. Therefore, this cannot have reference to Christ's reign for a thousand years upon earth.

2. A second Scripture is Psalm 110:1: "The LORD said unto my Lord, Sit thou at my right hand, until I make thine enemies thy footstool." That Scripture tells you that Jesus Christ, who is ascended into heaven and sits at God's right hand there, shall so sit there "till he hath made all his enemies his footstool." The apostle tells you that all Christ's enemies are to be made His footstool, so it cannot be till Christ's coming at the last time.

Will you mark that Scripture where the apostle tells you directly, 1 Corinthians 15:23–26: "But every man in his own order: Christ the firstfruits; afterward they that are Christ's at his coming. Then cometh the end, when he shall have delivered up the kingdom to God, even the Father; when he shall have put down all rule and all authority and power. For he must reign, till he hath put all enemies under his feet. The last enemy that shall be destroyed is death." Here is the coming of Christ that has reference to all the just and unjust. Mark now, Christ therefore must reign in heaven till all enemies are under His feet. Now [during] these thousand years all enemies are not under His feet. Why? Because death will be then; death is not to be destroyed then. When the end comes, He must give up His kingdom to His Father. What is more clear than this, that the heavens must keep Christ till all things be restored? And that cannot be till the day of judgment. Again, Christ must reign so long till the end of the world.

3. The third Scripture is 1 Corinthians 15:23–24: "But every man in his own order: Christ the first fruits; afterward they that are Christ's at his coming. Then cometh the end, when he shall have delivered up the kingdom to God, even the Father; when he shall have put down all rule and all authority and power." This Scripture tells you that when Christ comes out of heaven, upon Christ's coming, three things must be one: (1) Every man must rise, verse 23. Now that cannot be at the thousand years, because they themselves hold that there shall be only a resurrection of the martyrs, and there the Scripture says that every man shall rise, which cannot be till the day of judgment. (2) When Christ comes, then comes the end. The apostle tells us of His coming and the end of the world, to note that Christ's coming and the end of the world shall be together. (3) He delivers His kingdom up to His Father, whereas if Christ should reign a thousand years here it could not be said to be the giving up of a kingdom, but the taking of a kingdom into possession. He must resign all to God the Father. When the Scripture is so express, it is a wonder that men can receive such fantastic thoughts that Christ must come as an earthly monarch to reign here a thousand years.

4. A fourth Scripture is in Hebrews 9:28: "So Christ was once offered to bear the sins of many; and unto them that look for him shall he appear the second time without sin unto salvation." From that Scripture I will argue against Christ's coming to reign upon the earth for a thousand years: (1) It is expressly in

the Scripture that Christ's coming there spoken of refers to the day of judgment in verse 27: "And as it is appointed unto men once to die, but after this the judgment." There Christ's second coming refers unto the day of judgment. Now if the Scripture calls that the second coming which is His coming to judgment, then Christ cannot come before that time to reign upon the earth; for if He should come to reign upon the earth, then the apostle must call that His third coming. There has been but one coming, which was from heaven to the womb of the virgin, and there is no other coming to follow but a second coming, that is, to judgment. (2) It is said, Christ shall come the second time to our salvation; it cannot be said to our salvation if His coming were to reign a thousand years upon the earth; that were only some temporal good, but Christ's coming must refer to the last and great coming wherein the world shall be judged and the souls of the elect shall be saved. Beloved, these Scriptures are very clear unto me.

Problems with a Return before Judgment
The reasons are two that Christ shall not come personally out of heaven to reign upon the earth for a thousand years. First, because the Scripture manifests that when Christ comes personally out of heaven, there are [five] concomitants of His coming that can be referred to no other time than His last coming to judge the world.

1. When Christ is said to come out of heaven, the Scripture tells you this concomitant, that the saints shall come along with Him, Jude 14: "And Enoch also, the seventh from Adam, prophesied of these, saying, Behold, the Lord cometh with ten thousand of his saints." So that when Christ comes from heaven He must come with His saints with Him, nay, He must come with His angels, 2 Thessalonians 1:7: "And to you who are troubled rest with us, when the Lord Jesus shall be revealed

from heaven with his mighty angels." Put these two Scriptures together: Christ must come with His saints and angels. But those that fancy Christ's coming a thousand years cannot prove that Christ shall come with His saints and angels, for the Scripture that seems to carry it that way does not speak of angels and saints coming.

2. It is said when Christ comes from heaven that good and bad shall be gathered together, and all shall be judged by Jesus Christ. Now this cannot be of Christ's personal reign on the earth. This you have in 2 Thessalonians 2:1: "Now we beseech you, brethren, by the coming of our Lord Jesus Christ, and by our gathering together unto him." So that the coming of our Lord and our gathering together to be judged by Christ are both coupled together, because when the Lord comes, then is our gathering time, Matthew 25:31–32: "When the Son of man shall come in his glory, and all the holy angels with him, then shall he sit upon the throne of his glory: And before him shall be gathered all nations: and he shall separate them one from another, as a shepherd divideth his sheep from the goats." And 2 Timothy 4:1: "I charge thee therefore before God, and the Lord Jesus Christ, who shall judge the quick and the dead at his appearing and his kingdom." The Scripture tells you that when Christ appears to judge the world, He shall have this concomitant of His coming: "He shall gather all together to judge both the good and the bad." Those who pretend that Christ shall come to reign a thousand years upon the earth cannot prove that then all shall be gathered together. They only plead for the martyrs, and none else; therefore, it cannot refer to His coming to reign a thousand years.

3. When Christ comes then the end of the world is; a period is put to this world, 1 Corinthians 15:24: "Then cometh the end, when he shall have delivered up the kingdom to God, even the Father," &c. When Christ comes then comes the end. Now

those who hold for Christ's personal reign hold that the end of the world shall not be till a thousand years after, because Christ must reign a thousand years.

4. The resurrection both of the just and the unjust is a concomitant of Christ's coming, 1 Corinthians 15:23: "But every man in his own order: Christ the firstfruits; afterward they that are Christ's at his coming." So that at Christ's coming the general resurrection of the just and unjust is to be.

5. Lastly, there is to be the salvation of the souls of all the elect; that is a fifth concomitant of Christ's coming, Hebrews 9:28: "So Christ was once offered to bear the sins of many; and unto them that look for him shall he appear the second time without sin unto salvation." This cannot be referred to Christ's personal coming unto the earth to reign a thousand years, because He does not come then to save the souls of all the elect. That is the first reason why Christ cannot come to reign upon the earth, because when the Scripture speaks of Christ's coming out of heaven, it does not annex five concomitants with it, which belong not to any coming of Christ upon the earth but to come to judge the world.

A second reason is this, that Christ cannot come to reign upon the earth, because, if it should be so, it would be worse for Christ, and it would be worse for us than now it is. It would be worse for Christ to leave heaven and come to the earth, for Christ to leave saints and angels and heaven, to live upon the earth among the wicked and the good, for they themselves confess that wicked men shall live upon the earth then. Then besides, they fancy earthly delights, that the fruit of the vineyard shall not fade, as it now does, yet they would lessen Christ's glory because He sits this day at His Father's right hand. Again, for to fancy this, that Christ must come to reign upon the earth would be a great loss to all the elect, for we have the benefit of Christ's everlasting intercession. And were Christ upon the earth, we would lose that benefit, Hebrews 8:4: "For if he were on earth, he should not be a priest, seeing that there are priests that offer gifts according to the law." So that if He were upon the earth, we would lose the benefit of His priesthood. Therefore, it would be a great wrong to us to have Christ here on the earth, because the benefit of His priestly office would not be so available to us as it is in heaven.

Thus, I have laid down Scripture, and given you reasons why Christ cannot come before His last coming.

Incongruities of an Earthy Thousand-Year Reign
Now there are eight[5] incongruities and absurdities that would follow if you would grant that Christ should come to reign a thousand years upon the earth.

1. By those men's principles, this inconvenience will follow that people may exactly know the punctual time of Christ's last coming to judge the world; for those who hold Christ's personal reign do as well hold the time as the thing; they do as well maintain when this reign shall begin. Therefore, some have maintained that Christ should come to reign on the earth in the year 1650. One says if it shall not be in the year 1650, it shall be in the year 1694. They that go furthest guess at that time, if so be they hold the thing, and maintain the time also when it shall begin; then of necessity we must know exactly when the day shall be that Christ shall come to judge the world, for they grant it shall be immediately after the thousand years. Now beloved, that opinion that carries this absurdity, to know the day of Christ's coming to judge the world, which Christ said none in the world can tell, of that hour and day knows no man. Mark 13:32: "But of that day and that hour knoweth no man, no, not

---

5. Love mentions "eight incongruities and absurdities," but only cites seven.

the angels which are in heaven, neither the Son, but the Father," is a false opinion.

2. This incongruity will also follow: it will be a great disadvantage to Christ, in coming to reign a thousand years on the earth, to leave His Father, and heaven, and come and only possess earth. Now Christ has more happiness in the immediate enjoyment of His Father in heaven than He can have here upon the earth. Then it will be a loss to us that we should lose the benefit of His priestly office; but Christ, the Son of Righteousness, being in heaven is more available to believers than if He were upon the earth.

3. Observe this, that if Christ should come on the earth for a thousand years, then Christ would leave the church after that thousand years, for a while, in a worse condition than He found it. And I draw it from that text which they pretend to be the strength of their argument, Revelation 20:5, 7–8: "But the rest of the dead lived not again until the thousand years were finished. This is the first resurrection.… And when the thousand years are expired, Satan shall be loosed out of his prison, And shall go out to deceive the nations which are in the four quarters of the earth, Gog, and Magog, to gather them together to battle: the number of whom is as the sand of the sea." So that after the thousand years, the devil shall be let loose again; and there shall be an innumerable company of enemies, and they shall destroy multitudes of the godly. Therefore, Christ would leave His church in a worse condition than He found them if it were true that Christ should reign a thousand years upon the earth.

4. If Christ should come to reign a thousand years upon the earth, then this incongruity will follow: there must be three personal comings of Jesus Christ; for His first coming was His incarnation; second coming, to these thousand years. And His third coming must be to judge the world, that is, the last coming. But the Scripture makes but two comings of Christ: first, His

coming from heaven when He was born; His second coming when He comes to judge the world again.

5. If Christ comes personally out of heaven to reign a thousand years, this incongruity will follow, that either the saints and angels must come or not come with Christ. If they must come with Christ, then it is a loss to them to leave the immediate presence of God and come upon the earth where wicked men shall be among them. Or, if they must not come with Jesus Christ, yet it is a loss to them to remain there, for they shall lose for a thousand years the bodily presence of Christ. If Christ be on the earth, He cannot be in heaven at the same time. Therefore, it would be a loss to the saints and angels for them to be a thousand years in heaven without the company of Jesus Christ, not to have the person of Jesus Christ with them.

6. A sixth incongruity will follow, that if Christ shall come to reign upon the earth, then Christ's kingdom must be a worldly and terrene kingdom, and then it will be against the Word of God. He must be a visible king to the Jews, and a visible king to all the world. Besides, it would follow then that Christ's kingdom must not be a spiritual kingdom but a terrene, a worldly, pompous kingdom. John 18:36: "Jesus answered, My kingdom is not of this world: if my kingdom were of this world, then would my servants fight, that I should not be delivered to the Jews: but now is my kingdom not from hence." Luke 17:20: "And when he was demanded of the Pharisees, when the kingdom of God should come, he answered them and said, The kingdom of God cometh not with observation." Would not all the world observe Christ to come bodily from heaven and in the majesty of a monarch? Now Christ's kingdom does not come with observation. When the disciples looked after an earthly kingdom, "No," says Christ, "My kingdom is to rule and reign in your hearts. You shall never see Me to be an outward, pompous king in the world, for My kingdom is a spiritual kingdom."

7. That if Jesus Christ shall come to take a kingdom on the earth for a thousand years, then this would intimate, as if Jesus Christ had not a kingdom, and were not a king on earth all this while He is in heaven. They deny that place in Daniel, and all those phrases in the New Testament, that the kingdom of the world is become the kingdom of the Lord; they deny that Christ is a king in heaven. When He was in the manger and born in the stable, He was a king at that very hour, Psalm 2. The apostle refers it to Christ's birth and Christ's resurrection. Christ, when He arose from the dead, He was a king then, and the gospel under Christ's time is called a kingdom. It is remarkable in John 18:37: "Pilate therefore said unto him, Art thou a king then? Jesus answered, Thou sayest that I am a king." Christ was a king, though He would not be an earthly king to destroy earthly governments. Therefore, when the people in a tumult would have made Him a king, yet He would not. Zechariah 9:9: "Rejoice greatly, O daughter of Zion; shout, O daughter of Jerusalem: behold, thy King cometh unto thee: he is just, and having salvation; lowly, and riding upon an ass, and upon a colt the foal of an ass." He was king when He was on that slow, contemptible creature. So that now to say Christ shall come to reign as king is to intimate to the world as if Christ were not a king at this day, and whereas He is King of Kings, and Lord of Lords in heaven, therefore He cannot come a thousand years to reign upon the earth.

Revelation 20:2–6 Vindicated

Now I will deal fairly to show you the strongest Scripture that has most show of reason for the maintaining of this opinion and shall labor to take them off and clear it to you. There are multitudes of quotations that varieties of men's thoughts fasten upon to prove this point, yet those they most stand to I shall fasten upon. Their chief pillar is Revelation 20:2–6: "And he laid hold on the dragon, that old serpent, which is the Devil, and Satan, and bound him a thousand years…. And I saw thrones, and they sat upon them, and judgment was given unto them: and I saw the souls of them that were beheaded for the witness of Jesus, and for the word of God, and which had not worshipped the beast, neither his image, neither had received his mark upon their foreheads, or in their hands, and they lived and reigned with Christ a thousand years. But the rest of the dead lived not again until the thousand years were finished. This is the first resurrection. Blessed and holy is he that hath part in the first resurrection: on such the second death hath no power, but they shall be priests of God and of Christ, and shall reign with him a thousand years."

Problems with the Millenarian Interpretation
Now from this text, which is the chief Scripture for them, they seem to build these two things upon: First, that Jesus Christ shall live upon the earth, and the saints shall reign with Him for a thousand years. Secondly, those who were martyrs by antichrist shall rise from the dead and come upon the earth these thousand years to continue with Jesus Christ. This they build much upon, that Christ shall come to reign a thousand years upon the earth. But I shall show you that this cannot be the sense of it, and I shall give you six answers.

1. That though the Scripture says that the saints who were beheaded should live with Christ a thousand years, yet the text does not say that Christ shall come to reign with them a thousand years.

2. Though the text says that they should live and reign with Christ a thousand years, yet the text does not say that they shall reign with Him here upon the earth.

3. That though it be said that the saints shall live and reign with Christ a thousand years, yet living and reigning with Christ

does not necessarily imply them to be in the same place where Jesus Christ is, for then you would pervert many Scriptures. "For lo," says Christ, "I am with you to the end of the world." It does not therefore follow from that time He will be upon the earth to the end of the world, but Christ being with us, or we with Him, is by His Spirit. Romans 8:17: "And if children, then heirs; heirs of God, and joint-heirs with Christ; if so be that we suffer with him, that we may be also glorified together." The text does not denote the sameness of place and the oneness of situation. I give this to take off that which is made of this text.

4. It is evident that this Scripture cannot be a foundation to build on that Christ shall come to reign a thousand years upon the earth, because then it will not only follow that man shall live so long but shall reign with Christ so long on the earth. Methuselah lived but nine hundred sixty and nine years, and David said the life of man is cut shorter. The text says they shall live and reign with Christ, in that sense taking living properly, and all the phrases properly; they must necessarily say that men shall live when that time comes, a thousand years together. Again, it cannot be the sense of this Scripture, because that cannot be the sense of this Scripture that crosses the sense of other Scriptures, to make this Scripture to affirm that Christ shall reign on the earth a thousand years, and other Scriptures telling you that Christ shall stay in heaven in person till all men rise from the dead; every man shall rise; then comes the end. First Corinthians 15:23–24: "But every man in his own order: Christ the firstfruits; afterward they that are Christ's at his coming. Then cometh the end." Second Thessalonians 2:1: "Now we beseech you, brethren, by the coming of our Lord Jesus Christ, and by our gathering together unto him."

Then it crosses the Scripture to say that at Christ's coming only some men shall rise but not all. Job 14:10–12: "But man dieth, and wasteth away: yea, man giveth up the ghost, and where is he? As the waters fail from the sea, and the flood decayeth and drieth up: so man lieth down, and riseth not: till the heavens be no more, they shall not awake, nor be raised out of their sleep." Job tells you expressly that "the dead shall not be raised till the heavens be no more," and that cannot be the thousand years, for there will be an earth and a heaven then. In Peter's phrase, "The heavens shall melt away like a scroll," &c. Now to have a resurrection before a resurrection is that which the Scripture nowhere mentions. John 5:28–29: "Marvel not at this: for the hour is coming, in the which all that are in the graves shall hear his voice, And shall come forth; they that have done good, unto the resurrection of life; and they that have done evil, unto the resurrection of damnation." The judging of the just and unjust shall be the same hour, and upon Christ's coming all men shall be judged. Second Timothy 4:1: "I charge thee therefore before God, and the Lord Jesus Christ, who shall judge the quick and the dead at his appearing and his kingdom." So that Christ's appearing and Christ's coming is a judging of the quick and the dead. Now, beloved, to make this Scripture then to say that Christ shall come on the earth before His last coming is to cross other Scriptures. Then of necessity therefore it cannot be the scope of this, for there is no jarring between one phrase of the Scripture and another.

5. When the Scripture says here that they live and reign with Christ a thousand years, it is not spoken whether it is a reigning with Christ in heaven or on earth; so the phrase neither carries it one way or another.

6. John does not say that he saw the bodies of men who were beheaded and they reigned with Christ, but he did in a vision see the souls of those who were beheaded. Now to say they must come to reign on the earth for a thousand years, it were a great inconvenience to them. It is said, "I saw the souls of them." The thousand years cannot be applied to Christ's personal reign, for

so Jesus Christ has an eternal kingdom. He does not reign a thousand years on earth or in heaven but everlastingly. Kingdoms and states of this world have lasted a thousand years, and to make Christ's kingdom last no longer is to give Christ's kingdom too narrow a confine. I have consulted with many authors, and I find the current of interpreters generally run this way, though some fancy that the text speaks of the binding of the devil for a thousand years, and during this time the saints should live and reign with Christ a thousand years.

Defending a Better Understanding

The sense and scope of this place is this: The period of time when this time began that the devil was bound: interpreters unanimously give this opinion that the period of time that the devil was bound began in the reign of Constantine the Great,[6] he being the first Christian emperor in the world, he coming after three hundred years of persecution by the Roman emperors, who made great massacre and havoc in the church of God, insomuch that in *The Book of Martyrs*[7] we read that there may be, for every day in the year, five thousand Christians slain. This is a dreadful persecution, and the devil raged and stirred much. Now upon Constantine's reign the devil was bound up, that is, the Roman emperors, who were acted by the devil to all this cruelty; when Constantine, a Christian emperor, came to reign, he gave out imperial edicts and laws for establishment of the Christian religion, and that put an end to the persecution of the Roman emperors. And to this opinion many interpreters

---

6. Flavius Valerius Constantinus (ca. 280–337), known as "Constantine the Great," the first Roman emperor to profess Christianity.

7. John Foxe's *Acts and Monuments*, first published in 1563, a gigantic register of the persecution suffered during the English Reformation, swelling to over 2,300 folio pages in its second English edition.

give their consent (Brightman,[8] Napier, and Gerrard), and these thousand years when the devil was bound ended three hundred years ago and more, and this is given to be the scope and sense of the Scripture.

But then you will say, though the devil was bound, how does he come to be loose again? They answered that in the year 1300, the Turkish emperor began to bear sway. Gog and Magog, called the Turk, prevailed, and has gotten the greatest part of the world within his power. And he was the Gog and Magog that did persecute the saints, and spread almost over all the earth, and truly comparing Scripture and story together, this seems to be the nearest and the truest sense of this place, and this interpreters do generally concur in.

Two objections by those who plead for a thousand years. First, we read in the century of the church that the church of God was pestered by Valens the emperor after these three hundred years, and of Julian the Apostate,[9] who greatly persecuted the Christians, and how can this be true when we read of so much persecution after the devil was bound up? I answer, when it is said the devil is bound up, it is not meant simply that there should be no temptation to sin, for that there should be. Valens the emperor established Arianism and troubled the church of God. One answers it was nothing like the persecution under the Roman emperors; it was nothing so long nor so tedious as the persecution under the Roman emperors, for, for every day in the year, five thousand Christians were put to death.

---

8. Thomas Brightman (1562–1607), English clergyman, Puritan millenarian, and biblical commentator, whose commentaries on Revelation and Daniel were influential in spreading apocalyptic thought in the seventeenth century.

9. Flavius Claudius Julianus (331/2–363), a Roman emperor and nephew of Constantine the Great. He was raised as a Christian but later abandoned it in 351.

In Diocletian's[10] reign there were seventeen thousand Christians killed in one month. There was some sprinkling of persecution in the time of Valens and Julian the Apostate, but it was nothing to that of the Roman emperors.

Another objection is that the Scripture says that this is the first resurrection, that the saints living and reigning with Christ a thousand years, this is the first resurrection. How can it be said that after the time that the Roman persecution was curbed by Constantine that was a resurrection, and that they reigned with Christ at that time? For answer, first in Scripture phrase, the word "rising" does not carry a reference to the body rising from the grave only, but a man rising from a state of affliction and of sin. They are expressed in Scripture by a resurrection. Romans 11:10: "Let their eyes be darkened, that they may not see, and bow down their back alway." I say then, have they stumbled that they should fall? God forbid, but rather through their fall, salvation is come unto the Gentiles, for to provoke them to jealousy. Isaiah 22:19: "And I will drive thee from thy station, and from thy state shall he pull thee down." The men that are as it were low men in captivity in Babylon shall rise; it does not refer to the resurrection from the dead at the last day: so a rising from sin, Colossians 2:12: "Buried with him in baptism, wherein also ye are risen with him through the faith of the operation of God, who hath raised him from the dead." We are risen with Christ not bodily but out of our sins. Colossians 3:1: "If ye then be risen with Christ, seek those things which are above, where Christ sitteth on the right hand of God."

So that here this is the first resurrection. The meaning is that those that did escape the rage and cruelty of the ten persecutions, and did come to live in Constantine's days, and did all

---

10. Gaius Aurelius Valerius Diocletianus (284–305), a Roman emperor who oversaw the last major persecution of Christians in antiquity.

the while of the former persecutions keep themselves from the idolatry of the heathens and corruptions of antichrist are said to have the first resurrection. Blessed are they that were raised up by Christ from the sins, and from the errors, superstitions and idolatry, both of antichrist and the heathens.

Yes, but then it is said, they live and reign with Christ a thousand years. Beloved, that phrase, "living and reigning with Christ," though some interpreters refer it to heaven, yet with Brightman and others I concur, and also Bernard,[11] that it denotes this much: those in successive ages who enjoyed liberty in the Christian religion under Constantine the Great, who lived to a thousand years, and were delivered from former afflictions, who were kept by Christ's power from the idolatry of the times, and from antichrist, they were said to live with Christ a thousand years. For they lived to Him, and depended on Him, and were not plunged into the wickedness of the times. And thus with consulting of many authors, I find this to be the truest account, in a few words in defending this text from giving any foundation to Christ's personal reign for a thousand years upon the earth.

Vindicating Subsequent Passages
2 Peter 3:7–13
The second Scripture that they do urge for Christ's personal reign upon the earth for a thousand years is 2 Peter 3:7–13: "But the heavens and the earth, which are now, by the same word are kept in store, reserved unto fire against the day of judgment and perdition of ungodly men…. But the day of the Lord will come as a thief in the night; in the which the heavens shall pass away with a great noise, and the elements shall melt with fervent heat,

---

11. Bernard of Clairvaux (1090–1153), Cistercian monk and mystic whose writings deeply influenced the medieval church and reverberated throughout the Protestant Reformation.

the earth also and the words that are therein shall be burned up. Seeing then that all these things shall be dissolved, what manner of persons ought ye to be in all holy conversation and godliness, Looking for and hasting unto the coming of the day of God, wherein the heavens being on fire shall be dissolved, and the elements shall melt with fervent heat? Nevertheless we, according to his promise, look for new heavens and a new earth, wherein dwelleth righteousness."

Here is mention of a coming of Christ. We look for and hasten to His coming; at Christ's coming, we look for a new earth. Now say they, "To what purpose were there to be a new earth, if Christ were not to come down on this earth, and the saints with him for a thousand years, as the Scripture seems to give warrant for a thousand years reign: This Scripture seems to give warrant that He shall be on the earth; they say that the righteous shall only have benefit of Christ's personal reign upon the earth. To take this off,

1. Mark the scope and the context how this Scripture is brought in, and it will do something to clear the text. It is brought in against some Epicurean principles that some scoffers had taken up in those times, verses 3–4: "Knowing this first, that there shall come in the last days scoffers, walking after their own lusts, And saying, Where is the promise of his coming? for since the fathers fell asleep, all things continue as they were from the beginning of the creation." [That is,] we see no change in providence, therefore where is the promise of Christ's coming? They scoffed at Christ that He was a contemptible man in this world. This is the answer in the 7th verse: "But the heavens and the earth, which are now, by the same word are kept in store, reserved unto fire against the day of judgment and perdition of ungodly men." Peter speaks directly that the time of Christ's coming (which they scoffed at) was not the time of the thousand years but of the day of judgment. Therefore, this coming here

that Peter speaks of cannot mean a thousand years before the day of judgment.

2. Observe the day of perdition of ungodly men. They say themselves that Christ suffers the wicked of the world to live in the world the thousand years, though not to rule as they had done.

3. Observe that it is said here that before this new earth is the world shall be burnt with fire; the heavens shall pass away with a noise. Now before a thousand years there is no such thing since it is before the day of judgment. The burning of that world is reserved against the day of judgment; therefore, this coming cannot be referred to Christ's personal coming on the earth to reign a thousand years.

4. It is said here that Christ should come as a thief. "But the day of the Lord will come as a thief in the night, in the which the heavens shall pass away with a great noise," &c. That epithet refers to His coming to judge the world, to His last coming, and not to any other coming, 1 Thessalonians 5:2: "For yourselves know perfectly that the day of the Lord so cometh as a thief in the night." But if Christ should come to reign upon the earth, then He comes visible and observable. Matthew 24:43: "But know this, that if the goodman of the house had known in what watch the thief would come, he would have watched, and would not have suffered his house to be broken up." Therefore, be also ready, for in such an hour as you think not, the Son of man comes, Revelation 16:15, "Behold, I come as a thief. Blessed is he that watcheth, and keepeth his garments, lest he walk naked, and they see his shame."

5. And this divines stand much upon, it is said, "we, according to his promise, look for new heavens and a new earth, wherein dwelleth righteousness." That the dwelling of a righteousness here does not imply that such a thing shall be on the new earth, but the dwelling of righteousness refers to righteous men, not to

heaven or earth, the Greek word clears it plainly; it is a word in the plural number. Therefore, it is referred to the earth, which is in the singular number. Therefore, divines say, from the original, 2 Peter 3:13, "καινοὺς δὲ οὐρανοὺς καὶ γῆν καινὴν κατὰ τὸ ἐπάγγελμα αὐτοῦ προσδοκῶμεν, ἐν οἷς δικαιοσύνη κατοικεῖ"; "we in whom dwells righteousness, look for a new heaven, and a new earth." So that the dwelling of righteousness is not to be interpreted as referring to the earth but that righteousness should dwell in men; we read of none being on the earth, wherein dwells righteousness. Thus much for that other Scripture, "We look for new heavens and a new earth."

Daniel 2:44

A third Scripture, and that they deem to have some strength in too, [is] Daniel 2:44, "And in the days of these kings shall the God of heaven set up a kingdom, which shall never be destroyed: and the kingdom shall not be left to other people, but it shall break in pieces and consume all these kingdoms, and it shall stand for ever."

Now beloved, to give you the scope of the text, take these answers. (1) It is true that a kingdom is given by God to Jesus Christ, and that kingdom was given by God to Christ while He was here upon the earth in the form of a servant, and this Luke tells you, chap. 1, verses 32–33, "He shall be great, and shall be called the Son of the Highest: and the Lord God shall give unto him the throne of his father David: And he shall reign over the house of Jacob for ever; and of his kingdom there shall be no end." So that Jesus Christ had a kingdom, and He is now King of Kings, and Lord of Lords in heaven. (2) It is said here that this kingdom was begun in the days of those kings. Now whose days does this text speak of? It speaks of those that divided Alexander's kingdom, who overcame the Medes and Persians; it was divided between Ptolemy Lagides, King of Egypt, [and]

Zeleuchus, King of Assyria. In that time Jesus Christ set up a kingdom, for he was born King of the Jews. (3) It is apparent that this cannot be referred to Christ's kingdom in this world for a thousand years. Because it cannot be said that it should be a kingdom for ever and ever, for a kingdom for a thousand years cannot be said to be a kingdom for ever and ever, but it is said in Daniel, "It shall be for ever and ever."

Ephesians 5:5

A fourth Scripture is in Ephesians 5:5, "For this ye know, that no whoremonger, nor unclean person, nor covetous man, who is an idolater, hath any inheritance in the kingdom of Christ and of God." And this text Gerrard quotes and does well resolve it that they say there is not only a kingdom of God that is heaven, but the Scripture makes mention of a kingdom of Christ as a kingdom of God. Therefore, they build on Christ's reign, and of having a kingdom here upon earth. (1) I answer, it is true, Christ has a kingdom, but He says expressly that His kingdom is not of this world, John 18:36, "Jesus answered, My kingdom is not of this world," &c. (2) Though it be said here that there is a kingdom of Christ, yet it is not expressed to be upon the earth for a thousand years. (3) This kingdom of Christ interpreters refer it to the same with the kingdom of God, and [it is] to be meant exegetically.

Matthew 26:29

A fifth text they have is in Matthew 26:29, "But I say unto you, I will not drink henceforth of this fruit of the vine, until that day when I drink it new with you in my Father's kingdom." Alsted[12] quotes from thence they gather it cannot be meant of heaven.

---

12. Johann Heinrich Alsted (1588–1638), Reformed minister, academic, encyclopedist, and polymath, whose wide-ranging interests led to a variety of influential publications in the seventeenth century.

Why? Because there is no eating and drinking there; here is a promise by Jesus Christ to come to them no more, till He would drink with them wine in His Father's kingdom, and it cannot be unless Christ comes in person amongst His people; and have a kingdom to eat and drink with His people in this world. This they stand much upon.

Take these clear answers to these quotations: (1) This cannot be meant of a kingdom in this world for a thousand years. My reason is this: because the kingdom, which is Christ's personal reign, should be called Christ's kingdom, and not His Father's kingdom; it should have been called "My kingdom," and not "My Father's kingdom"; that is one answer that divines give. (2) Observe that this may refer to that time between Christ's resurrection and ascension, for after Christ rose from the dead, you know He continued forty days upon the earth, and the Scripture tells you, in Luke 24:42–43, "And they gave him a piece of a broiled fish, and of an honeycomb. And he took it, and did eat before them." So He may as well drink and eat, but to me [it] is somewhat uncertain. (3) Which is the true scope of this place, "I will not drink henceforth of this fruit of the vine, until that day when I drink it new with you in my Father's kingdom" [Matt. 26:29]. He was taking the Lord's Supper, and was drinking the cup of wine. Says He, "I am going away, and will drink no more till we meet in heaven; not that there should be eating and drinking in heaven, but when you and I meet, we shall have sweet fellowship and communion together, as is in eating and drinking together." As feasting is a badge of communion and love, so there shall be endeared love and endeared communion with Christ in heaven. You shall drink it new, not new wine, nor eat new bread but after a new manner of love and communion. They should express love to each other, and have everlasting communion one with another.

They say likewise that there shall be no sin in the world, and that the earth shall be restored to its primitive fruitfulness as it were before the fall; but I shall not meddle with these. And thus, according unto my poor measure, I have labored to lay down the grounds from Scripture why Christ cannot come to reign personally upon the earth a thousand years and have vindicated those Scriptures that seem to patronize that opinion.

Application of Christ's Spiritual Reign

Is it so that the Scripture does not determine any coming of Christ out of heaven till His last and great coming to judge the world? O, then, labor to make it your work to have Jesus Christ as king to reign in your hearts by mortification, to rule in your heart by His Spirit, to mortify your headstrong lusts that are in you.

Secondly, seeing there is no coming of Christ as king in this world, then labor to have Christ to reign in His church by a well-ordered discipline, that the government of Christ may be established in the places where you dwell.

Thirdly, seeing there is no coming of Christ as king in this world, then do not trouble yourselves with niceties and obscurities about His coming upon the earth, but labor to be fitted and prepared for His last and great coming.

Fourthly, if Christ should come to reign upon the earth (which the Scripture in no way speaks of), then certainly the saints of these times make a bad preparative for Christ's reign who impale saintship and monopolize saintship unto themselves, and say they are the people of God, the church of Christ, and the saints of Christ. They make a bad preparation for Christ's coming to live in sensuality as they do, and commit such wickedness as they do upon the earth.

This is but a bad preparation and poor encouragement to Jesus Christ to come and reign amongst such saints as these are, who indeed are a scandal to saints, a scandal to religion, and would be a scandal to that thousand years of Christ, if He should come to reign; but Christ will have better saints than these are to reign with Him.

CHAPTER 6

The Manner of Christ's Second Coming

In treating the doctrine of Christ's coming again, the other query is this: How or after what manner shall this coming of Christ be? "But I will come again." Now in the resolving of this question, I shall confine my answers to these six particulars: First, He shall come certainly. Secondly, He shall come personally. Thirdly, He shall come visibly. Fourthly, He shall come gloriously. Fifthly, He shall come terribly. And sixthly, He shall come unexpectedly. These ways the Scripture furnishes you with several hints touching His coming.

The Circumstances of Christ's Return

First, the Lord Jesus shall come certainly. Christ's coming is not to be numbered among poetic fictions, or with the delusion of Mohammed. The certainty of Christ's coming again is built on these three foundations:

1. It is built on the immutability of God's decree, Acts 17:31, "Because he hath appointed a day, in the which he will judge the world in righteousness by that man whom he hath ordained; whereof he hath given assurance unto all men, in that he hath raised him from the dead." The immutability of God's decree proves the certainty of Christ's coming; God has appointed a day in which He will judge the world.

2. The certainty stands upon the infallibility of Christ's promise. Matthew 26:64: "Jesus saith unto him, Thou hast said: nevertheless I say unto you, Hereafter shall ye see the Son of man sitting on the right hand of power, and coming in the clouds of heaven." There is Christ's promise, to which three of the evangelists concur.

3. It is grounded upon the impartiality of His justice. Here every man has not justice, and in Solomon's phrase, "A just man perisheth in his uprightness, and a wicked man prolongeth his days in wickedness." Therefore, to show God's impartiality, there must be a coming of the Son of Man to judge the world righteously. The doctrine of Christ's coming is impugned by atheists; therefore, you read what Peter tells you, 2 Peter 3:3–4: "Knowing this first, that there shall come in the last days scoffers, walking after their own lusts, And saying, Where is the promise of his coming? for since the fathers fell asleep, all things continue as they were from the beginning of the creation." And we read that the men of Athens questioned this and would not believe that Christ would come to judge the world, Acts 17:32: "And when they heard of the resurrection of the dead, some mocked: and others said, We will hear thee again of this matter." Of old time, in the times of Jesus Christ, or soon after, men mocked at the doctrine that the dead shall rise, and Christ would come to judge both the quick and the dead. Herein Gerrard reckons up an abundance of sects, such as the Floriani, the Dosithiani, the Symmachiani, and many others. Indeed, there is one Scripture that these atheists abuse in making it deny the coming of Christ to judgment: John 8:15, "Ye judge after the flesh; I judge no man."

But, beloved, to this text that they use to shake this great pillar of our hopes, the coming of Christ again, take these two answers: (1) When Christ said, "I judge no man," that is, "I judge no man with a rash and heady judgment, as you judge men who are not of your opinion. You judge things rashly and inconsiderately, but I judge no man as you do." So Augustine, in his thirty-sixth tract on John, gives this sense of the place [that] it does not exclude Christ from judging the world at the last day but from judging of men as the Pharisees, to wit, rashly and inconsiderately. (2) Christ here speaks what was not the end of His first coming in the flesh but the end of His second coming to judge all men. "I judge no man," that is, "It was not the intent or the end of My first coming in the flesh to judge men" (John 3). When God sent His Son to be born of a virgin, He did not send Him to judge the world but to save the world; He reserved His judging of the world till His last coming. John 12:47–48, "And if any man hear my words, and believe not, I judge him not: for I came not to judge the world, but to save the world. He that rejecteth me, and receiveth not my words, hath one that judgeth him: the word that I have spoken, the same shall judge him in the last day." [As if He had said,] "The end of My first coming was not to judge; it was to be judged, and to be condemned by Pontius Pilate, and to die the cursed death." And that is the vent of Christ's first coming; that is the first particular: He shall come certainly.

Secondly, Christ shall not only come certainly, but He shall come personally. It was the great mistake of Origen (though he holds for the coming of Christ again) that he pleads for the coming of Christ in Spirit; therefore, that text where it is said, "You shall see the Son of man coming in the clouds of heaven," Origen understands the clouds to be the saints, because it is mentioned in Scripture that the believers are called a cloud of witnesses. Now this is to pervert the whole letter of the Bible and turn all the Scripture into an allegory and metaphoric sense.

Now in opposition to that, I lay down a second property, that Christ's coming shall be a personal coming out of heaven, but the Scripture does not speak of Christ's coming on the earth but no further than the air. Christ in His body shall come personally out of heaven.

Now to prove this second property, or second manner or way of Christ's coming, there are two texts of Scripture to confirm it. 1 Thessalonians 4:17: "Then we which are alive and remain shall be caught up together with them in the clouds, to meet the Lord in the air: and so shall we ever be with the Lord." Verse 16: "For the Lord himself shall descend from heaven with a shout." If it had been Christ in His Spirit, then it would have been said the Lord by His Spirit shall descend. [But it says,] "The Lord Himself shall descend from heaven with a shout." It notes His personal coming out of heaven, that whereas Jesus Christ had a personal translation, and as Christ had a visible elevation, He was in the eyes of His disciples lifted up, so Christ shall bodily descend and come out from heaven, the Lord Himself, &c. Therefore, it cannot be the Lord by His Spirit. Acts 1:11: "Which also said, Ye men of Galilee, why stand ye gazing up into heaven? this same Jesus. which is taken up from you into heaven, shall so come in like manner as ye have seen him go into heaven." The same Jesus that you saw ascend shall descend, so that it cannot be Christ in His Spirit but in His person. I only mention this to confute those who follow the conceit of Origen, merely making Christ's coming to be but a spiritual coming, a coming in the hearts of saints.

Thirdly, His coming shall be visibly, Acts 1:11: "This same Jesus, which is taken up from you into heaven, shall so come in like manner as ye have seen him go into heaven." That as Christ's going up to heaven bodily was visible, so Christ's coming out of heaven shall be visible. Matthew 26:64: "Hereafter shall ye see the Son of man sitting on the right hand of power, and coming in the clouds." Indeed, Christ rose invisibly, for no man saw Christ rise from the dead; but Christ shall descend visibly.

You shall see the Son of man. Matthew 24:30: "And then shall appear the sign of the Son of man in heaven: and then shall all the tribes of the earth mourn, and they shall see the Son of man coming in the clouds of heaven with power and great glory." All men shall see the glory of Jesus Christ. The wicked shall see Him to their amazement and consternation, and the godly shall see Him to their joy and consolation.

Fourthly, Christ's coming shall be glorious, and there shall be many things that shall make the coming of Christ to be a glorious coming. He shall come in the clouds. These glorious bodies shall be triumphant and swift chariots of the Son of God, wherein He will come to judge the world. And His attendance shall make Him glorious, Daniel 7:10, "A fiery stream issued and came forth from before him: thousand thousands ministered unto him, and ten thousand times ten thousand stood before him: the judgment was set, and the books were opened." Jude 14: "And Enoch also, the seventh from Adam, prophesied of these, saying, Behold, the Lord cometh with ten thousands of his saints." Second Thessalonians 1:7: "And to you who are troubled rest with us, when the Lord Jesus shall be revealed from heaven with his mighty angels." O, then, behold the clouds to be the triumphant chariots of Christ, the innumerable company of saints and angels to be attendants on the person of Christ to come to judge the world, and that is the reason that He is called so glorious, Matthew 24:30: "And they shall see the Son of man coming in the clouds of heaven with power and great glory." Matthew 16:27: "For the Son of man shall come in the glory of his Father with his angels." Luke 9:26: "For whosoever shall be ashamed of me and of my words, of him shall the Son of man be ashamed, when he shall come in his own glory, and in His Father's, and of the holy angels." And that is the reason of that epithet given to Christ's coming [in] Titus 2:13: "Looking for that blessed hope, and the glorious appearing of the great God and our Saviour Jesus Christ."

Now beloved, Christ's coming to have this property or this manner, the reason must be to distinguish His second coming from His first coming; to take off the contempt and reproach that was on Jesus Christ in His first coming, and He shall come in glory in the second coming. First, we read in Scripture that Christ's first coming was in the form of a servant. Philippians 2:7: "But made himself of no reputation, and took upon him the form of a servant, and was made in the likeness of men." Now in the second coming, He comes with the glory and majesty of a king. In the first coming He had no reasonable creature to attend Him; at the second coming, He shall have all the saints and angels in heaven to attend Him. At His first coming, He was swaddled with swaddling bands, but at His second coming, He shall be, as it were, clothed with the clouds of heaven. Again, His first coming was in dishonor and contempt; every traveler had more honor than Jesus Christ, for the inn was for every traveler, but there was no room for Christ there. He was born in an outhouse; but His second coming shall be in great glory. Again, in His first coming, Christ, representing the persons of the elect, came with sin imputed to Him, and was the greatest beggar in the world, as Luther said. He was the greatest sinner in the world not by way of inheritance but by way of imputation; therefore, Luther called Him *peccator maximus*, the greatest sinner. Christ, in coming into the world, had all the sins of the elect of God imputed to Him; so He came as a sinner, as an evil person, though He was not so, yet He was looked upon as so. But the second time He shall come without sin. He shall not have our sins by imputation cast on Him, because when He comes again He shall make a total abolition of sin. Therefore, there needs be no imputation of our sins upon Jesus Christ. Thus, you have a fourth way of His coming: He shall come gloriously.

A fifth way of Christ's coming again is this: He shall come terribly. Isaiah 13:9: "Behold the day of the Lord cometh, cruel both with wrath and fierce anger, to lay the land desolate: and he shall destroy the sinners thereof out of it." Revelation 6:17: "For the great day of his wrath is come; and who shall be able to stand?" The coming of Jesus Christ is a terrible coming.

Sixthly, and lastly, Christ shall come unexpectedly. Though it is true, there shall be immediate warnings of His coming, as the powers of heaven shall be shaken; the sun, moon, and stars shall be darkened but that shall be but a little before His coming. But, beloved, the coming of Christ shall be when men are not aware of it, as in the days of Noah men were eating and drinking and marrying and giving in marriage when the flood came and destroyed them. So shall the Son of Man come. Christ's coming shall then be to burn all with fire. When men shall be eating and drinking, possessing, and adding store to store, when men are secure and never think of Christ's coming to burn all with fire, then the powers of heaven shall be shaken and the world be set on fire. Hence it is that you read in Scripture in five or six places, "Christ's coming shall be as a thief in the night." A thief will come in the dead time of the night, as Christ said to His disciples in Luke 21:34. The coming of Christ is an unexpected coming. Thus, you have six particulars of Christ's coming.

Terrifying Applications of Christ's Return

Now a word of application. Having shown you how this doctrine of Christ's coming is a doctrine of comfort, I shall finish this point by showing you how this doctrine of Christ's coming is a doctrine of terror and of dread, and to whom. It is observable the Word is not compared only to milk and honey, but the Word is compared also to salt, which also has an efficacy to cause pain. Beloved, you have heard the honey of this doctrine, what great comfort it will afford to godly men, but remember, the Word is salt also, and it is of a painful efficacy to terrify and fret the conscience. Now the doctrine of Christ's coming is a terrible doctrine in these things:

[First,] to all wicked men, Christ's coming again is a terrible doctrine because all the secret sins that ever a wicked man has committed in this world shall be made manifest to all. I confess it is a contest among learned men whether the sins of good men as well as bad shall not be known, and there are strong arguments that all shall be made known; but the Scripture is full in this: at the day of judgment, the sins that a wicked man has done in this world shall be published to all the saints and angels in heaven, and all the men who were on the earth. It may be, you go for an honest man among your neighbors, yet you love your neighbor's wife and go in unto her. If you have been so, or you have deceived in your trade, why, for all your secrecy here, yet then all the world shall know your deceit and uncleanness. It is built upon that text, Luke 8:17: "For nothing is secret, that shall not be made manifest; neither any thing hid, that shall not be known and come abroad." Here a thousand things are hidden that men do not know; here you carry it fairly and squarely in the world, so that men cannot say, "Black is your eye." But then they may say, "Shame to your face"; this is dreadful.

Secondly, Christ's coming shall be dreadful in regard of your separation from all the elect of God. In Matthew 25:32–33: "And before him shall be gathered all nations: and he shall separate them one from another, as a shepherd divideth his sheep from the goats. And he shall set the sheep on his right hand, but the goats on the left." Here you are mingled; it may be you live in the same house with a godly man, and lie in the same bed with a godly man; but remember, a parting time is coming. As the shepherd parts the sheep from the goats, so Christ parts the wicked from the godly.

Thirdly, Christ's coming again is dreadful to wicked men in that it shall be the time of the promulgation of your sentence. A thief in Newgate prison is a miserable creature; a thief at the bar is in a sad condition, but a thief when the sentence of death is passed upon him is in a hopeless condition. O you wicked man, at your dying day you are a malefactor, but at the giving of your sentence you are an undone man; you are in a hopeless condition.

Fourthly, Christ's coming is the time of the reuniting of your body and soul together, and of your taking possession of hell. When your body and soul that have been so many hundreds of years parted shall come to meet together, and your meeting is but to go into infernal torments; this makes the coming of Christ to be a dreadful coming.

"Yes," but you will say, "it is true indeed. A Felix may tremble when Paul shall preach to him of judgment to come, but have we Christians cause of fear?" Yes, you who are Christians, if you are found under these particulars that I am now naming to you, the day of judgment will be dreadful to you. Christ's coming again to judge the world is not only a dreadful doctrine to a Felix, but may make you, a Christian, to tremble in these cases.

First, the doctrine of Christ's coming may make men tremble who are guilty of acts of oppression and violence in courts of judicature. Ecclesiastes 3:16–17: "And moreover I saw under the sun the place of judgment, that wickedness was there; and the place of righteousness, that iniquity was there. I said in mine heart, God shall judge the righteous and the wicked: for there is a time there for every purpose and for every work." That is, to judge every purpose and every work. When God shall come to places of judgment and places of judicature, and shall say, "Wickedness is there," and shall say, "Bribery is there, and the deferring of the cause of the poor is there," woe be to all oppression of the poor, and grinding their faces in courts of judicature, many whereof are seats of violence and not courts of judicature.

Christ shall come to judge things that men will not judge. Men will not judge adulterers, but "whore-mongers and adulterers God will judge." Men will not judge men for heresy, but God will judge them. Christ's coming is dreadful to all men who live by oppression and violence in courts of judicature.

Secondly, Christ's coming to judgment is dreadful to all those who, to save their worldly advantage, are ashamed to profess the gospel of Christ. O! Christ's coming is a dreadful time to these. In Mark 8:38: "Whosoever therefore shall be ashamed of me and of my words in this adulterous and sinful generation; of him also shall the Son of man be ashamed, when he cometh in the glory of his Father with the holy angels." I pray you, mark here are two answers to an objection in these words. First, men might say, "Why, blessed Jesus, who would be ashamed of Thee? If Christ were on the earth, we would never be ashamed of Christ!" Therefore, Christ adds, "Whosoever is ashamed of me and of my words." Though you might not be ashamed of Christ's person, yet you might be ashamed of His words.

Then men may object and say, "Why, truly, if it were a peaceable time, a safe time to profess Christ; but what, when we live in a wicked place, and among a wicked people, will not Christ bear with us, to hold down our heads a little, and to sleep in a whole skin?"

"No," says Christ, "whosoever shall be ashamed of me and of my words in this adulterous and sinful generation, of him also shall the Son of man be ashamed." Let the place be never so bad, you must not be ashamed of Jesus Christ and His words. If you are, the Son of Man shall be ashamed of you when He comes with the glory of His Father. Christ's coming is dreadful to all you who are ashamed to profess Jesus Christ in the sinful and adulterous age and place wherein you live. I shall leave it to you to make application.

Thirdly, Christ's coming to judgment is dreadful to all those who spend their days in sensuality and riot. [Christ's] coming is terrible to them, Luke 21:34: "And take heed to yourselves, lest at any time your hearts be overcharged with surfeiting, and drunkenness, and cares of this life, and so that day come upon you unawares." Men who live in riot, excess, and sensuality do but pamper their flesh and feed themselves to make themselves a sweeter morsel both for worms and devil. Christ's coming will be a dreadful time for them.

Fourthly, Christ's coming will be dreadful to all those who bear not a sincere love to Jesus Christ. Will you mark one Scripture? for First Corinthians 16:22: "If any man love not the Lord Jesus Christ, let him be Anathema Maranatha." There is much of God's mind in this dark expression. "If any man love not the Lord Jesus Christ, let him be an accursed man," that is the meaning of the word "anathema." But the other word, "maranatha," is a word compounded of two words, and it bears this sense: "Maran" signifies "a Lord," and "atha" signifies "venit; He comes"; so then, when the Scripture says, "He that loves not the Lord Jesus Christ, let him be an accursed man, let him be Maranatha," [it is to be taken that] when the Lord Jesus shall come to judge the world, let Christ then curse him that does not love Him. O, then, I beseech you, think this with yourselves, that all you who do not bear a sincere love to Jesus Christ when He comes, His coming shall be with a curse, a curse to hell and damnation to all such.

Fifthly, Christ's coming will be dreadful to all those who obstinately refuse subjection and obedience to the gospel of Jesus Christ. Second Thessalonians 1:7–8: "And to you who are troubled rest with us, when the Lord Jesus shall be revealed from heaven with his mighty angels, In flaming fire taking vengeance on them that know not God, and that obey not the gospel of our Lord Jesus Christ." Christ's coming will be in a flaming fire to take vengeance on all such.

Sixthly, Christ's coming will be dreadful to those who live and die railers against religion. To those who scoff and jeer at godliness, Christ's coming will be a dreadful coming. Jude 15: "To execute judgment upon all, and to convince all that are ungodly among them of all their ungodly deeds which they have ungodly committed, and of all their hard speeches which ungodly sinners have spoken against him." I do wish it were engraved before the eyes of all wicked railers. There is many a railing Rabshakeh, and many a cursing Shimei, who have uttered many a hard speech against the people of God. They accuse one man to be a hypocrite for carrying a Bible under his arm, and another man of being a hypocrite for shedding a tear in his sermon. O you are the men that Christ will come to execute judgment upon, to convince you of your hard speeches.

Seventhly, to unmerciful men Christ's coming is a dreadful time. James 2:13: "For he shall have judgment without mercy, that hath shewed no mercy." Christ's coming to judgment shall be a time of your having judgment without mercy, who show no mercy. Matthew 25:41–43: "Then shall he say also unto them on the left hand, Depart from me, ye cursed, into everlasting fire, prepared for the devil and his angels. For I was an hungered, and ye gave me no meat: I was thirsty, and ye gave me no drink: I was a stranger, and ye took me not in: naked, and ye clothed me not: sick, and in prison, and ye visited me not."

Augustine has a good gloss upon this text. Says he, "If that man shall go to hell that will not give another man bread when he is hungry, O then to what a hell shall that man go to which takes away bread from the hungry man! And if that man shall go to hell that will not clothe the naked, O then to what a hell shall that man go to that takes clothes off the necessitous man's back! And if that man shall go to hell that will not visit men who are in prison, O then to what a hell shall that man go to that casts godly men into prison!" Now, beloved, I beseech you to take heed that you are not men wanting bowels of mercy towards your distressed brethren. You are to expect judgment without mercy that show no mercy.

Eighthly, to those who live and die in their sin of uncleanness and lusts of the flesh, Christ's coming will be a dreadful day to them. Therefore, you read that God will judge adulterers. He will judge a drunkard. He will judge a swearer. He will judge a Sabbath-breaker, yet particularly whoremongers and adulterers He will judge. Hebrews 13:4: "But whoremongers and adulterers God will judge." King Henry the Eight was a lascivious prince, and old Latimer sent him a token, a Bible, and about the Bible was written, "Whoremongers and adulterers God will judge." It was to terrify him.

There is a strange text in 2 Peter 2:9–10: "The Lord knoweth how to deliver the godly out of temptations, and to reserve the unjust unto the day of judgment to be punished: But chiefly them that walk after the flesh in the lust of uncleanness." Here is a "chiefly" for them: God will punish every unjust man, but God reserves them to the day of judgment, "chiefly them that walk after the flesh in the lust of uncleanness." Do I speak to men who may have this "chiefly" applied to them? O take heed that you do not fall under the righteous judgment of God, that you are not entangled in that sin that will make the Lord judge you chiefly.

Ninthly, and lastly, Christ's coming again is dreadful to all men who strengthen themselves by popular tumults and insurrections in opposing and destroying a lawful magistracy, that have destroyed judges, rulers, and governments; it will be a woeful time to them, 2 Peter 2:9–10: "The Lord knoweth how to deliver the godly out of temptations, and to reserve the unjust unto the day of judgment to be punished: But chiefly them that walk after the flesh in the lust of uncleanness, and despise government.

Presumptuous are they, selfwilled, they are not afraid to speak evil of dignities"; [that is,] men that under pretense of power and the like shall trample down rule, government, authority, and dignity. The Lord has another day to judge those who will not be judged here. He will judge them with a "chiefly." And thus I am done with the third doctrine.

CHAPTER 7

The Reception of Souls at Death

I am now to make entrance into the fourth fundamental doctrine in these words, "And receive you to myself." These words contain in them that great fundamental point touching the resurrection of man's body, that not only the soul shall go to heaven, but also the bodies of the godly men shall go to heaven. Christ shall come out of heaven for this end, to receive the bodies as well as the souls unto Himself. "I will come again and receive you to myself."

There is some difference between interpreters touching the sense of these words. One carries it this way: that here the promise of Christ's coming, made a little before He was to die, refers not to the last coming; but they refer it to that forty days that He was upon the earth after His resurrection to the ascension. They say that this promise was accomplished when Christ, after His resurrection, came to His disciples and ate a broiled fish with them, and stayed forty days with them. Why? What comfort would this be to the disciples to think of Christ's going away and coming again, and staying but forty days and then to be seen no more? This would have made them the more sorrowful that they should never have seen Him more.

Here are two or three reasons from the text why that cannot be the sense of the place, because here was a promise before that He was going to His Father's house to receive them there.

Now that living upon the earth forty days after His resurrection cannot be His Father's house. This cannot therefore mean Christ's coming again at that time to them. Again, it is said where He was to go: He was to prepare a place for them. Now if His meaning had been that He would come again in forty days, it would have been an earthly place that He had prepared for them; but the current of interpreters, seeing the weakness of that, give many consequent reasons why it must necessarily be referred to Christ's last coming and everlasting receiving of them, when the body shall be raised, and at that coming He has promised the elect that He would receive them unto Himself; [it is] as if He should have said, "Though I leave your bodies behind Me in the world for a season, though they may be mangled and massacred by cruel persecutors, and though you may be without My bodily presence for a while, yet I do not go to heaven to stay there forever. But I promise you, I will come again, and then I will take you into heaven with Me." They would fain have had Christ to have received them into heaven, and that they might have gone with Him. The disciples, when they heard Christ speak of going to His Father's house, they were all on fire to go with Him into heaven. "O, no," said Christ, "I will come again to judge the world, and then I will receive your very bodies into heaven with Me, that as My body is in heaven, so your bodies shall be there also with Me."

The observation is this: that it is one great end of Christ's coming again to receive the bodies of all the elect unto Himself into heaven with Him. "I come again, to receive you unto Myself." I shall not follow the common place in handling the resurrection of the body. I shall only handle this point practically in showing you what the happiness of the elect of God is in their bodies as well as their souls. Now because this text is used to pervert many Scriptures, I shall handle this practical question before I come to handle the doctrine.

Refuting the Doctrine of Soul Sleep

The question is this: that seeing Jesus Christ does only promise that He will receive the elect unto Himself at His coming again, then what becomes of all the godly immediately after death, before Christ's coming again to judgment? Those that hold for the sleeping of the soul on this text ground that there is no receiving, neither one or other, the one to life, the other to death; the wicked are not tormented till then, nor the godly glorified till then. Therefore, it is needful that, seeing Christ here speaks of receiving them unto Himself not till His coming, to show what becomes of the souls of dead men before the coming of Christ.

Before I give you the answer, take this distinction: there is a twofold receiving. First, there is a partial and incomplete receiving, and this is done immediately after death, that when the soul departs from the body the soul is received by Jesus Christ into heaven, and that is the reason for those speeches in Acts 7. There is a receiving of them before Christ's coming, and this is called a partial and incomplete reception; it is only a receiving of the spirit, and not of the body. Second, there is a total and complete reception both of the body and soul into glory, and it is this that the text here speaks of. Though it is true, there is not a total reception of a believer till Christ's coming to judgment, yet there is a partial reception. I do not now speak to those that say the soul is mortal, and that it shall never live after the death of the body but to those that say the soul shall sleep and the soul perishes with the body until the resurrection.

Now against these that plead for the sleeping of the soul till Christ's coming again, take these four ways how to strengthen you. First, there are *pregnant instances* in the Scripture that after the godly die their souls are received into heaven before Christ comes. Secondly, there are *general expressions* in the Scripture, as well as particular instances to prove this. Thirdly, there are *express passages* in the Scripture to confirm this. Fourthly, there are *absurd inconsequences* that will arise in case it should be denied.

Examples of Souls Going to Heaven

First, there are *pregnant instances*, or examples in the Scripture to prove that after death the soul is received into heaven. Take three instances.

1. That known text, Luke 23:43, "And Jesus said unto him, Verily I say unto thee, Today shalt thou be with me in paradise." That day Christ died, that day Christ went to heaven; therefore, that day the soul of that converted thief did go to heaven.

Now, beloved, there are two evasions that those who plead for the soul's cessation, for the soul's sleeping, make to avoid this text, and take off this instance. [A] first [evasion] is by altering the comma or stop in the text, and read it thus, "I say unto thee this day, thou shalt be with me in paradise"; that "today," they do not refer it that the thief should be in paradise. Peter Martyr gives two answers to this evasion. (1) Says he, it is not safe to alter a comma or stop in Scripture, for so you may pervert the Scripture and make it say what it never meant, if men at their pleasure, disagreeing from all copies, alter the commas in the translation. (2) Another answer, that it appears this cannot be the sense of it, to refer "today" to the time that Christ spoke, and not the time that the thief should be in heaven; for, says Gerrard, mark the thief's prayer in verse 42: "And he said unto Jesus, Lord, remember me when thou comest into thy kingdom." Mark, there is the thief's *when*, that *when Christ should come to heaven*. Christ should remember him. Christ's *hodie* must answer to his *quando*, or else He did not answer his prayer. Christ's "today" must answer the thief's "when," that *when* Christ came to heaven, then to remember the thief. "And Jesus said unto him, Verily, I say unto thee, Today shalt thou be with me in paradise." It is needless for Christ to say "today" to tell him the time when

He spoke. He knew Christ spoke to him then; but to speak of the time when the thief would be in heaven was needful. "I say to thee this day thou shalt be with Me in heaven."

The second evasion is this. It is true, Christ promised, "thou shalt be with me in paradise," but Christ does not say, "thou shalt be with Me in heaven." There are three answers to confute this evasion: (1) That those that will not by "paradise" understand heaven by this text, they then fall in with the papists, either for purgatory or a *Limbus Patrum*. (2) Take this answer, that in other Scriptures when paradise is mentioned, it is to be understood "heaven," and so the apostle expounds it, 2 Corinthians 12:2, 4: "I knew a man in Christ above fourteen years ago, (whether in the body, I cannot tell; or whether out of the body, I cannot tell: God knoweth;) such an one caught up to the third heaven.… How that he was caught up into paradise, and heard unspeakable words, which it is not lawful for a man to utter." So that the apostle, by "paradise," means heaven, Revelation 2:7: "He that hath an ear, let him hear what the Spirit saith unto the churches; To him that overcometh will I give to eat of the tree of life, which is in the midst of the paradise of God." That is, he shall enjoy Jesus Christ. Christ in heaven is the tree of life in the paradise of God. (3) It cannot be an earthly paradise, as the paradise Adam was in before his fall, for the earthly paradise was destroyed by the flood. Therefore, of necessity, when Christ tells the thief, "Today thou shalt be with me in paradise," it must refer to the thief's going to heaven that day with Jesus Christ.

2. A second instance is in Luke 16:22: "And it came to pass, that the beggar died, and was carried by the angels into Abraham's bosom: the rich man also died, and was buried." This is another instance where the souls of the elect after death go to heaven.

There are two evasions made upon this text. First, they say that this text is a parable and not an historical narration. To this

I answer, though some men say it is a parable, yet many say it is a history. Jerome, and many following him, give many arguments to prove that it was a history, and not a parable. Tertullian is confident that this is an exact history of what was really done. And Peter Martyr[1] quotes Tertullian; says he, Tertullian is so confident that this is an history that he undertakes to tell you who were the men; says he, the rich man was Herod, and the beggar was John the Baptist. But suppose it be a parable and not a history; yet parables do carry the resemblance of truth. Parables take their foundations from truth: that there are some men in hell and some men in heaven; that in hell there is torment and in heaven there is joy; that as the beggar went to heaven after death, so shall the godly, and as the rich man went to hell, so shall all the wicked. The other evasion is that this beggar is said to be carried into Abraham's bosom. I answer, first, it is more than probable that Abraham's bosom is heaven. Now Abraham, being in heaven, all his children are in heaven that are in his bosom. That is the answer that Gerrard gives. Again, it is said that they are carried by angels into Abraham's bosom; therefore, Abraham's bosom must be in heaven. Certainly, the good angels carry a good soul into heaven, and the wicked angels carry a damned soul into hell. And thus you have two instances that immediately after death the souls of the elect go to heaven.

3. A third instance is in Matthew 22:31–32: "But as touching the resurrection of the dead, have ye not read that which was spoken unto you by God, saying, I am the God of Abraham, and the God of Isaac, and the God of Jacob? God is not the God of the dead, but of the living." I argue from that instance that therefore Abraham, Isaac, and Jacob were living at that time, though

---

1. Peter Martyr Vermigli (1499–1562), Italian Calvinist reformer known for his teachings on the Eucharist. He became a professor in divinity at the University of Oxford during the reign of Edward VI but was exiled upon the ascent of Queen Mary in 1553, after which he became a professor of Hebrew in Zurich.

not in their bodies. If you mark the reason of that text, it was not to prove a resurrection of the body only, which the Sadducees deny but also to prove the immortality of the soul. The Sadducees deny spirits and angels too, Acts 23:8: "For the Sadducees say that there is no resurrection, neither angel, nor spirit: but the Pharisees confess both." Christ proves that there shall be a resurrection of the body, and He likewise proves that the soul does not die when the body dies. Indeed, there is a quotation that I have read of a learned man who makes use of this instance, Genesis 25:8: "Then Abraham gave up the ghost, and died in a good old age, an old man, and full of years; and was gathered to his people." Abraham was not gathered to his fathers, nor to be gathered in the grave where his forefathers were; how then can this be true that the Scripture says, "Abraham was gathered unto his fathers"? Divines say that it must be in his soul, that Abraham went to heaven as his godly forefathers went; that is the meaning of that phrase. His soul was to be bound up in the bundle of life, to go to heaven as their forefathers did. And thus much for particular instances.

Statements Suggesting Souls Go to Heaven

The second way to prove that the souls of the elect men go to heaven immediately after death: it is by general expressions in Scripture. Two general passages, one is Hebrews 12:23: "To the general assembly and church of the firstborn, which are written in heaven, and to God the Judge of all, and to the spirits of just men made perfect." Thence I argue that apostle makes mention, and proves, that these were the spirits of just men made perfect. Now if their souls perished with their bodies, then the apostle should say that their spirits are annihilated with the body, but it is "the spirits of just men made perfect." The Scripture takes notice in general expressions that just men have their souls made perfect. And then there is Ecclesiastes 12:7: "Then shall the dust return to the earth as it was: and the spirit shall return unto God who gave it." Mark, here are two things. Here is the end of godly men: "the body shall go to the dust, and the soul to God." Then the time when it shall be is when that man goes to his long home, when the keepers of the house shall tremble, that is, the hands and arms; and the strong men shall bow themselves, that is, the feet and the thighs; and the grinders shall cease, that is, the teeth; and they that look out at the windows shall be darkened, that is, the eyes. When nature decays, and the body perishes by diseases, and dies, "then shall the body go to the dust, and the spirit to God that gave it."

Passages Confirming Souls Go to Heaven
Thirdly, I shall prove it to you from express passages in the Scripture that do confirm this, that the souls of the elect after death before Christ's coming are received into heaven. For this I will give four or five express Scriptures.

1. The first is in John 6:40: "And this is the will of him that sent me, that every one which seeth the Son, and believeth on him, may have everlasting life: and I will raise him up at the last day." Here are two distinct promises: a promise of everlasting life, [and] a promise of raising up at the last day. A promise of everlasting life is made distinct from the other. Divines say that before the raising up at the last day there is an everlasting life, that his soul shall live before the last day, and his body shall be raised up at the last day.

2. Another text is in Luke 16:9: "And I say unto you, Make to yourselves friends of the mammon of unrighteousness; that, when ye fail, they may receive you into everlasting habitations." Chemnitz[2] makes great use of this text to prove what I am now

---

2. Martin Chemnitz (1522–1586), an eminent second-generation German Lutheran, known as "the second Martin," who worked tirelessly to achieve

arguing for, that immediately after death the soul of an elect man is received into heaven. Mark, "make you friends of the mammon of unrighteousness," that is, of your wealth, called so either because it is unrighteously gotten or unrighteously kept. Use your wealth well, "that when you die, you may be received into everlasting habitations." It is questionable whether it refers to angels, or to the poor, which shall pray for us that we be received into heaven; but, says Chemnitius, use your wealth well, that you may be received into everlasting habitations upon your failing, upon dying the Lord receives the elect into everlasting habitations. This Chemnitius builds on, that the soul goes to heaven immediately after death.

3. A third Scripture is in Philippians 1:23: "For I am in a strait betwixt two, having a desire to depart, and to be with Christ, which is far better." The apostle joins these two conclusions: a departing out of the world, out of this life, and a desire to be with Jesus Christ. He mentions no middle place for a good soul to go to. He mentions neither purgatory nor *Limbus Patrum*.

4. And so likewise a fourth text you have in 2 Corinthians 5:6: "Therefore we are always confident, knowing that, whilst we are at home in the body, we are absent from the Lord." We are confident, I say, and willing rather to be absent from the body and to be present with the Lord; wherefore we labor that whether present or absent we may be accepted of him. Mark, the apostle, desires to be absent from the body and to be present with the Lord, so that the soul is present with the Lord while absent from the body.

5. Then again, that prayer of Stephen proves it likewise, in Acts 7:59: "And they stoned Stephen, calling upon God, and saying, Lord Jesus receive my spirit." It had been uncomfortable

doctrinal harmony within German Lutheranism, which was achieved by the Formula of Concord (1577).

for him to have thought that he should have been stoned for Jesus Christ, and it must have been above 1600 years before Christ should have received his soul; but he prayed, "Lord Jesus Christ, receive my soul," which he would not have done if he had not believed that his soul would have been received by Jesus Christ immediately after death.

And thus I leave those Scriptures to confirm you in this, that the soul does not sleep in the body, but at the departure from the body it does immediately go to heaven.

Absurdities of Denying Souls Go to Heaven
[Fourthly,] I prove it to you by showing those gross absurdities and inconveniences that will arise if it should be denied that God does not receive the soul of any elect man till He comes to judge the world.

1. It will follow that the godly will be in a worse condition after they are dead than they were in when they were alive, for when they were alive to live was Christ. Christ dwelt in their hearts by faith. Now if the soul does sleep with the body, and perish with the body, then Christ does not live in them. Christ does not dwell there by faith; so that this would be uncomfortable that a believer after death should be in a worse condition than during this life, for here he lives in Christ by faith.

2. Then it will follow that God the Father would be more cruel to His people than He would have other men be to their servants which have done their work. Mark Leviticus 19:13: "Thou shalt not defraud thy neighbour, neither rob him: the wages of him that is hired shall not abide with thee all night until the morning." That the master was not to keep the hire of the laborer long from him, that the master should not keep the servant's wages long from him. Now will the great God keep from you who are His servants, that have served Him here in this world, and have done Him faithful service, any reward till

His last coming? No, but when you have ended your life and done your work, you receive your wages; when your work is done, you will have your reward.

3. Observe this, if it should be true that the souls of elect men do not go to heaven after death, then it will follow that the souls of wicked men do not go to hell after death, and how repugnant this is to the Scripture you well know, when the Scripture says in the Epistle of Jude that the men of Sodom and Gomorrah suffered "the vengeance of eternal fire." Acts 1:25: "That he may take part of this ministry and apostleship, from which Judas by transgression fell, that he might go to his own place." I could give you a multitude of instances where it is shown the wicked are in hell. First Peter 3:19–20: "By which also he went and preached unto the spirits in prison; Which sometime were disobedient, when once the longsuffering of God waited in the days of Noah, while the ark was a preparing, wherein few, that is, eight souls were saved by water." To say that a godly man does not go to heaven immediately after death, it will follow that a wicked man does not go to hell immediately after death.

4. It would follow that there should be only angels in heaven and no saints, whereas the Scripture says expressly that Christ shall come from heaven with His saints. And we read in Scripture that there are "the spirits of just men made perfect," as well as "the innumerable company of angels."

5. It would follow that it would be a great discomfort to a godly man on his deathbed to think he should be so many hundred years, soul and body in the grave, before Christ would bring him to heaven. It would be a very uncomfortable doctrine for a man to think on, that I shall die like a beast, that my soul after death shall not be taken up into heaven. And thus I have proved that immediately after the godly die, their souls are received into heaven. I have proved it by pregnant instances in the Scripture, by general expressions in the Scripture, and by

those express passages in Scripture, and have given you those absurdities that will arise it case it should be denied.

Application of Souls Going to Heaven

A word now from what has been spoken. If it be that Christ does receive you, O believer, to Himself before the total and complete reception, I would then give you this use to comfort you.

Fear not your dying time. Let not death be dreadful and terrible to you. Beloved, were it true indeed that when you die your soul should perish with your body, then a life is not the worth having. But when you shall think on your deathbed, "Here now is a disease consuming my body and sending me to my grave, and now there is but a little time between me and heaven, that when I am a dying, I am in the very suburbs of heaven, a little breath between me and heaven," O how should this comfort a dying man, when he has good evidences for heaven! O this should greatly comfort you when you come to die, to think that your deathbed is the very suburbs of heaven.

I have read what John, that wrote the Revelation, when he was ready to die [said]: "I do believe," says he, "that in this very day my soul shall be presented before the Lord Jesus Christ." O think, now you are leaving your friends, "it will not be a day before Christ and I shall meet in heaven." As in the *Book of Martyrs* we read that in Queen Mary's time, two friends were put to death together. One of them was fearful to think that the flames should scorch his flesh. O, says the other, "be of good comfort, for half an hour hence thou shalt be in heaven!" O think, though you are weak and sick even unto death, yet that you shall shortly be with Jesus Christ. O doubt not the truth of this. For I could even pawn my soul of the truth of it, that the souls of the elect are taken up into heaven immediately after death. O then, let not death trouble you.

CHAPTER 8

The Resurrection of the Body

The fourth doctrine here mentioned is the benefit of Christ's coming, and that is to raise your bodies from the dead and receive them to Himself. This is the particular that I am now to insist upon, "and receive you to myself." The observation is this, that the main end of Christ's coming again is to raise the bodies of the elect, and to receive them to Himself, not only to save the soul immediately after death, but to raise the body also. There are two queries in the doctrinal part of this point touching the end of Christ's coming, which is to raise the bodies of the elect, and to receive them to Himself. First, why Jesus Christ must raise the bodies of the elect, and receive them to Himself, as well as the souls. Secondly, when Christ does receive the body to Himself, then what endowments does the body receive as now it has not?

Reasons for the Resurrection

First, why must Christ receive the body to Himself, as well as the soul? There are four reasons.

1. Because of the resurrection of His own body. Christ's body is raised from the dead and received up into heaven, and therefore the bodies of the elect must be there also. Where Christ is, there must His members be. Christ the head is raised from the

dead and received up into glory. The apostle gives this reason, 1 Corinthians 15:12, "Now if Christ be preached that he rose from the dead," &c. As if he should have said, Christ being risen from the dead argues that our bodies must rise from the grave, though they be dead there. In 1 Corinthians 6:14, "And God hath both raised up the Lord, and will also raise up us by his own power." First Thessalonians 4:14, "For if we believe that Jesus died and rose again, even so them also which sleep in Jesus will God bring with him." So that because Jesus Christ's body is raised from the dead, and received up into heaven, therefore our bodies must be raised up and received into glory with Him.

2. The bodies of the elect must be raised because of the inhabitation of the Spirit. The Spirit sanctifies the bodies of the elect as well as their souls. [1 Thess. 5:23], "And the very God of peace sanctify you wholly; and I pray God your whole spirit and soul and body be preserved blameless unto the coming of our Lord Jesus Christ." First Corinthians 6:18–20: "Flee fornication. Every sin that a man doeth is without the body; but he that committeth fornication sinneth again his own body. What? know ye not that your body is the temple of the Holy Ghost which is in you, which ye have of God, and ye are not your own? For ye are bought with a price: therefore glorify God in our body, and in your spirit, which are God's." Now the Spirit of God having a gracious work in the body as well as the soul; therefore the body must be raised up from the dead as well as the soul. And for this the Scripture makes an argument of the resurrection in Romans 8:11: "But if the Spirit of him that raised up Jesus from the dead dwell in you, he that raised up Christ from the dead shall also quicken your mortal bodies by his Spirit that dwelleth in you." So that Spirit that raised up Christ from the dead, if that dwells in you, and the graces of the Spirit, that Spirit shall quicken your mortal bodies; therefore, the bodies of

the elect shall be raised from the dead and received into glory with the soul.

3. Because the body has a conjunction and cooperation with the soul in all gracious working, the body shall be partner with the soul, being received up unto Jesus Christ, because the body does cooperate with the soul, Romans 8:13: "For if ye live after the flesh, ye shall die: but if ye through the Spirit do mortify the deeds of the body, ye shall live." Now being that the godly do mortify the deeds of the body, and do expose their bodies to tortures and torments for Jesus Christ; now because the bodies of the elect do cooperate with the soul in good, therefore the body shall be co-partner with the soul in good also.

4. It proceeds from that near union which is between a believer and Jesus Christ. Christ is the head and believers are the members. Now the members must be raised and received up to Jesus Christ to make His body a perfect body. Thus much for the reasons why that Jesus Christ at the second coming shall raise and receive the bodies of the elect to Himself as well as the souls.

Benefits of the Resurrection

The second query is this: but what benefit is it to the body, what endowments shall the body receive by this when Christ comes? First, in general I shall say this to you, that the body shall receive more glorious endowments than ever it could be capable to receive and enjoy here in this world. It may be your body is endowed with a comely feature; yet when Christ comes to receive your body it shall be endowed better than now it is. Chrysostom[1] says, "Take wool, and let this wool be dyed into a scarlet, or purple color, dyed in grain, yet the wool is the same

---

1. John Chrysostom (347–407), early church father, biblical commentator, orator, and archbishop of Constantinople, whose gifts in preaching earned him the name "golden-mouthed."

wool as it was before, when it was white; but yet there is a more goodly lustre put upon it." Your body shall be the same body, but the body shall have more illustrious endowments than now it has.

And thus much only in the general; [I] now come to particulars. I shall resolve this question in these six particulars. There are six glorious endowments that the body shall receive from Jesus Christ at His second coming when He receives the body to Himself.

1. From being a natural body as it is now, it shall be made by Christ a spiritual body; that is the first endowment. You shall cast off your old apparel of corruptible flesh and blood, and shall be clothed with robes of glory. It is no contradiction to say a "spiritual body," because the apostle uses the expression, 1 Corinthians 15:44: "It is sown a natural body; it is raised a spiritual body. There is a natural body, and there is a spiritual body." The meaning is [that] the body as it lives here is a natural body, needing natural refreshments; but, says the apostle, "it shall be raised a spiritual body." The meaning is [that] the body as it lives here is a natural body, needing refreshments; but, says the apostle, "it shall be raised a spiritual body"; it shall have no more need of natural refreshments, which the natural body requires. When it is a spiritual body, it stands in no more need of meat, no more need of drink, nor sleep and other natural refreshments; it shall be raised a spiritual body. Matthew 22:30: "For in the resurrection they neither marry, nor are given in marriage, but are as the angels of God in heaven." The angels have no need of food, and stand in no need of outward helps, Revelation 7:15–16: "Therefore are they before the throne of God, and serve him day and night in his temple: and he that sitteth on the throne shall dwell among them. They shall hunger no more, neither thirst any more; neither shall the sun light on them, nor any heat." Therefore, O believing soul, behold your happiness of soul and

body in glory. They shall be no more standing in need of natural refreshments than spirits do; when the Scripture says that your bodies should be received by Christ. The platonic philosophers understand [it to mean that] the body shall be turned into a spirit, into a ghost, or into wind or air; but that is not the reason of it. It shall be of the same substance as it is upon the earth, but it shall be refined.

2. The bodies of the elect, when Christ receives them to Himself, of vile bodies, they shall be made beautiful. It may be you have some deformity, but Christ shall refine that body, apply new varnish and make it beautiful, Philippians 3:21: "Who shall change our vile body, that it may be fashioned like unto his glorious body, according to the working whereby he is able even to subdue all things unto himself." The body of Christ is a beautiful body, neither spot nor wrinkle, nor any such thing in it. Your body shall be like Christ's glorious body. First Corinthians 15:43: "It is sown in dishonour; it is raised in glory: it is sown in weakness; it is raised in power." Here your body is a vile body. Eliphaz calls the body a house of clay, and Job calls it a house of earth.

It is the opinion of Gerrard, and he gives strong reasons for it, that if there are any defects upon the body in this world, if any of the members of the body be wanting, it shall be restored to you at the resurrection, and there are these reasons to be given for it: (1) Because our bodies are promised to be like Christ's body. Now Christ's body has no redundant and defective member. Defect is the product of sin and the result of sin; therefore our bodies, being said to be like Christ's body, there shall be no defect in it. (2) Some members are necessarily required to make up the happiness of the elect in heaven. Suppose an elect man should be born blind or lose his eyes by casualty. If this man should not have his eyes, he could never see Christ in heaven. We shall see with these very eyes the body of Christ. (3) The third reason is this, because the bodies of the elect shall be as Adam's body was in innocency. Adam's body was created perfect by God. When Christ raises your body, it shall never want a member nor abound in a member. Your vile body shall be beautiful. What if others are fairer than you, and clearer skinned than you? What though other men's earth is painted better than yours? Yet when Christ receives your body, it shall be a beautiful, a glorious body. Therefore, you have that phrase, Matthew 13:43: "Then shall the righteous shine forth as the sun in the kingdom of their Father."

3. From being a mortal body, it shall be made by him an immortal body. The body, as it is here, is a mortal body dying and rotting in the grave; but it shall be made by Christ immortal, 1 Corinthians 15:52–53: "In a moment, in the twinkling of an eye, at the last trump: for the trumpet shall sound, and the dead shall be raised incorruptible, and we shall be changed. For this corruptible must put on incorruption, and this mortal must put on immortality." Those mortal bodies that must die must be made immortal, and those corruptible bodies made incorruptible, and never die. This is the great happiness of the elect, that their bodies shall be made immortal bodies.

4. The bodies of the elect, from being liable to sorrows and sufferings in the world, shall be made impassive bodies. The body here is exposed to diseases, aches, consumptions, and what not. The body is a hospital of diseases, a magazine of all infirmities; but the Lord shall make this body impassive, liable to no sufferings. God shall then wipe away all tears from our eyes—no sorrows, no crying, nor no pain. There is the great happiness of the body: it shall be made impassive, not liable to hunger, thirst, disease, and the like.

5. Your body, from being a heavy and lumpish body as now it is, shall be made an agile and swift body. The eagle shall not flee so strongly, as the bodies of the elect shall flee from place to place. It is grounded from that Scripture, 1 Thessalonians 4:14:

"For if we believe that Jesus Christ died and rose again, even so them also which sleep in Jesus will God bring with him." Which the body could not do if the body did not lose its lumpishness and heaviness which it has here. Zanchy illustrates it by this comparison; says he, the body is like the chick in the egg; the bird in the egg strives not; but when it is flushed, then it can fly. So, when you are raised, you can go from one part of the world to another in a moment. So was Christ's body when it was raised. Christ was taken immediately up into heaven, which is, as astronomers say (if we may believe their guesses), above forty millions of miles. Now the soul has a lumpish body that it cannot follow the soul; therefore, the body shall be made conformable to the soul; the body is now a tired jade to the soul, but then it shall not be so.

6. From being a weak body, it shall be made a strong body, 1 Corinthians 15:43: "It is sown in dishonour, it is raised in glory: it is sown in weakness; it is raised in power." The body of man is a weak fleshly thing. Anselm is of this opinion on this text, 1 Corinthians 15. Says he, man's body shall be so strong that he shall be able to toss a mountain as a child would toss a tennis ball. This is the great glory that God puts on the body, that, being a natural body, it shall be made by Christ a spiritual body; of being a vile body, it shall [be] made by Christ a beautiful body; from being a mortal body, it shall be made an immortal body; from being liable to sorrows and sufferings in this world, it shall be made impassive; being a heavy lumpish body, it shall be made an agile body; and from being a weak body, it shall be made a strong body.

Answering Objections against the Resurrection

Now before I come to the application, there are two objections that lie in the way. As in the primitive times, there were the Sadducees that held there was no resurrection, and after Christ's time there was Hymeneus and Philetus, which said that the resurrection was past already, and the church of Corinth was tainted: "If Christ is risen from the dead, how say some amongst you, that there is no resurrection of the dead?" Now in the primitive and Christ's time there was the opinion that there was no resurrection of the body, and so made this merely but a poetic fiction, and to be no real and undoubted truth.

The Scripture which they urge is this. "You talk of the body being raised by Christ, but how can this be when the apostle says expressly that the body is made of flesh and blood? First Corinthians 15:50: 'Now this I say, brethren, that flesh and blood cannot inherit the kingdom of God, neither doth corruption inherit incorruption.' Therefore, if flesh and blood cannot come to God's kingdom, how then can the body come there?"

First, I answer that it cannot be the apostle's intent to impugn the body's rising, for the drift of the whole chapter is to prove that the body shall be raised. Therefore, it is not imaginable that in one breath the apostle should envy and affirm the same thing.

Secondly, the apostle understands by "flesh and blood" the bodies of men, as they have sinful infirmities, cleaving to them in this world. The body, as it is now a sinful body, an infirmed body, a weak mortal body as it is now, shall never come to heaven. The generality of interpreters run this way. By "flesh and blood" is understood the bodies of men as liable to sin. In this world they shall not be raised up; they shall not come to heaven, but we shall be changed. We shall not all sleep, but be changed. The apostle proves this in 1 Corinthians 15:50–51: "Now this I say, brethren, that flesh and blood cannot inherit the kingdom of God, neither doth corruption inherit incorruption. Behold, I shew you a mystery: We shall not all sleep, but we shall all be changed." Our corruptible bodies shall not come to heaven as they are corruptible, but come to heaven by being incorruptible. "But we shall all be changed," that is, our bodies shall be changed from being mortal, corruptible, and being weak and sinful, to be holy and immortal. So that flesh and blood as now it is sinful and corruptible, till changed and made glorious and pure, shall not come to heaven.

[A] second text which they urge against the body being glorified, and say it is but a fancy, [is] Job 14:7–10: "For there is hope of a tree, if it be cut down, that it shall sprout again, and that the tender branch thereof will not cease. Though the root thereof wax old in the earth, and the stock thereof die in the ground; Yet through the scent of water it will bud, and bring forth boughs like a plant. But man dieth and wasteth away: yea, man giveth up the ghost, and where is he?" A tree, says Job, if that dies it may live again; but if man dies, he vanishes away, and where is man? On this they build that man shall never live again.

To this, take this clear answer: That when Job says, "Though a tree dies, it lives again; but if man dies, he lives not," Job understands it to mean living again in this world, so there is more hope of a tree than of a man.

But you will ask me, "How do you prove this to be Job's intent?" I prove it to you from Job's words in the 12th verse: "So man lieth down, and riseth not: till the heavens be no more, they shall not awake, nor be raised out of their sleep." So that here Job speaks of a rising when the heavens shall be no more, when the world shall be burnt with fire; then man shall be awakened. And in the 14th verse: "If a man die, shall he live again? all the days of my appointed time will I wait, till my change come." Job speaks in this chapter of the change of the body and of the raising of the body. Tertullian and Augustine say well that there is no doctrine of religion more repugnant to sense and reason.

There is this reason that may seem to be against the raising of the body. How is it possible that the bodies of men can be raised when that they are so confounded together as they are in the earth? Suppose a man be killed and devoured by a wolf, a lion eats that wolf; suppose that the lion dies, and the fowls of the air eat that lion, and men eat those fowls. How can the bodies of men be raised, being thus confounded? Suppose a man is drowned in the sea, and the fishes in the sea eat that man. How can his substance be gathered together at the last day?

It is the answer of Perkins.[2] First, much may be done by nature, by art. First, take an illustration from a refiner. Put before a refiner a mass of metal, and there shall be in that one lump a vein of silver, a vein of brass, of gold, of tin, or iron, and the like, and these metals are all mingled together. Now a refiner, by his art, can distinctly sever the silver from the gold and the iron from the lead. Now can art do this, and shall not the God of nature sever this man from that man? God shall sever them though they are heaped together.

Again, a gardener sows a variety of seeds. If you come to the garden, and one asks you what seed lies in that bed or in this bed, as rotting in the ground, you cannot tell; but come to the gardener and ask him what seed is in that bed, and he can tell you distinctly the seed in every bed. And cannot the great God do this? He who made us knows our shape. We cannot tell what man's dust this is in the grave; yes, but God that laid it in the grave, He knows. He knows which shall be my dust and which shall be your dust, and which every man's dust. He knows what body shall spring up thence. Therefore, labor to exalt faith in the great mystery of raising and glorifying your bodies.

Applications of the Doctrine

I have now a practical application to make of this. The uses.

---

2. William Perkins (1558–1602), English Reformed pastor and theologian, often referred to as "the Father of Pietism." Perkins's writings heavily influenced seventeenth-century Puritanism.

First this, is it so that Jesus Christ shall raise your bodies and receive them to Himself at His second coming? Then let this comfort you against your sufferings in the body. Suppose you are exposed to violent sufferings, to torments, tortures, to racks, fire, and faggots. Suppose your body undergoes this for the sake of Jesus Christ; yet remember, your body shall be raised and glorified by Jesus Christ. Let it not trouble you, then, that your body shall be a crucified body, because at Christ's second coming it shall be a glorious body. Again, it may be comfort to you by reason of your natural infirmities. Suppose your body be a sickly body; suppose your body is full of aches, agues, consumptions, diseases, and the like; suppose your body be maimed, blind, and lame; yet remember, your body that is vile, deformed, and sickly. It shall have fresh robes of glory upon it, and be made like the glorious body of Jesus Christ.

We read in the *Book of Martyrs* of two martyrs who were to be burnt at Stratford-Bow near London: Hugh Laverock and John Apprice, the one blind and the other lame.[3] Apprice was full of fear when the fire was about him. Hugh said unto him, "Be not troubled; though you are blind and I lame, yet remember death will heal you of your blindness and me of my lameness." Suppose you are blind, lame, and maimed, Christ's receiving of your body will cure all. And truly there were comfort to a man under a bodily distemper when a man should think that this body of mine should rot in the grave, and never be raised from the dead. But your deformed body should be a beautiful body. That which is a sickly body shall be made a healthy body and freed from all diseases.

A second inference is this: will Jesus Christ at His coming raise your body and receive your whole man unto Himself?

---

3. John Foxe, *Acts and Monuments* (1570), 2090. Laverock and Apprice were martyred on May 15, 1556.

Then learn to have a thirsting and longing soul after the second coming of Jesus Christ. Do not desire to continue here upon earth, but to be dissolved and to be with Jesus Christ. Will any man be grieved for changing an old suit for a new? Death does this; you have here an old rotten rag of flesh about you. Christ will put a new suit on you. Therefore, the apostle calls it the desire of the body to be clothed upon. We do not desire to be in heaven without bodies, but we desire to be clothed with those glorious endowments wherewith the elect shall be clad in glory. Therefore, be not unwilling to die; do not be unwilling to leave an old rotten carcass, a sickly body, a diseased body. Put a bird into a cage, and though the cage is made of silver or gold, yet the bird would rather fly abroad than be tied up in the cage. While in the body you are in a cage. You would rather have your body in a glorified capacity than now it is.

Thirdly, be not afraid or unwilling to die, because your body shall be changed by death. If your body should not die, it would never be a glorified body. Keep your corn in your house and you will never have a crop, but cast your corn into the ground and let it die here, says the apostle, that you sow is never quickened till it die. Let your body be kept alive here in the world and it shall never be raised to glory. O, do not then be unwilling to die, because death to an elect man is as a laying of corn in the earth. As corn rots in the ground to spring again against the harvest, so your body rots in the grave to spring again at the resurrection.

Fourthly, if it is true that Jesus Christ will raise your body unto glory, O then do not abuse these bodies of yours. They are the temples of the Holy Ghost. These bodies of yours shall one day be raised and received by Jesus Christ. It is an argument that the apostle raises in 1 Corinthians 6:14–15: "And God hath both raised up the Lord , and will also raise up us by his own power. Know ye not that your bodies are the members of Christ? shall I then take the members of Christ, and make them the members of an harlot? God forbid." This is the apostle's argument. The apostle would reason against adultery and uncleanness in the body. What argument does he use? "Know ye this, Christ will raise up our bodies, and shall we take these members of our bones, and make them the members of a whore?"

So then, beloved, let the doctrine of your resurrection, and of your bodies being raised and received to Jesus Christ, provoke you that you do not abuse your bodies. He who keeps company with a harlot sins against his own body, 1 Corinthians 6:18: "Flee fornication. Every sin that a man doeth is without the body; but he that committeth fornication sinneth against his own body." For a man to lie and swear is against his soul; but for a man to be unclean is to sin against his body. O, do not die with an unclean body, with an adulterous body. And do not abuse your body; do not abuse those eyes of yours to be windows of lust that shall one day behold Jesus Christ. Do not abuse that body that must have a sweet communion with Christ in heaven.

CHAPTER 9

Everlasting Communion with Christ

I am now come to handle the last point in the text, the last clause, "that where I am, there you may be also." These words note unto you the event or consequent what shall follow upon Christ's coming again and receiving our bodies unto Himself at the last day. The event shall be an everlasting enjoyment of Christ. That is the result and consequent of Christ's coming: to be ever with Him, that "where I am, there you may be also."

Being There with Christ

I shall open the words, for there is some difficulty in that one expression "where I am." You see, it is a word in the present tense, "where I am"; and though it is a word of the present tense, it does not denote that they should be at Jerusalem with Christ (for Christ was then at Jerusalem); but as Grotius said that here the word of the present tense is to be understood of the future tense, that is, "where I shall be shortly after I leave this world; where I shall be, there you shall be." And so He brings that text to prove it, John 7:34: "Ye shall seek me, and shall not find me: and where I am, thither ye cannot come." It cannot be taken in the present tense, for He was then at Jerusalem, but it is to be understood in the future tense, "where I shall be, I go, but I come again, that where I shall be when I come to My Father's house in heaven, I may have all your companies to be personally present with Me in heaven." That is the scope of the word.

Observe that whenever Christ speaks of being in heaven, though He was on the earth, yet He speaks in the present tense, as if He were in heaven already. John 3:13: "And no man hath ascended up to heaven, but he that came down from heaven, even the Son of man which is in heaven." Christ was not in heaven. He was speaking on earth to them in His person, in His human nature. So likewise in John 17:24: "Father, I will that they also, whom thou hast given me, be with me where I am; that they may behold my glory, which thou hast given me; for thou lovedst me before the foundation of the world."

Gerrard raises this question here: "Why does Christ say that He is in heaven, when yet He was in His body on the earth?" First, that Christ says, "I am," denotes the certainty of Christ's going to heaven, that He should be there as sure as if He were there. [For instance,] Babylon is fallen, [but] the popedom is not fallen, [and] yet it shall be as sure as if it were fallen. It is to note, secondly, the suddenness of it. Christ was shortly to be in heaven; there was but one day between Christ and His being in heaven. Things suddenly to be done are said to be done; things that are near doing are said to be done. Thirdly, which is the reason that Gerrard gives, Christ expresses it in the present tense, "where I am," though He were on earth, to show that Christ was truly God as well as man, and in regard of His divine nature He was truly in heaven, as in regard of His human nature He was on earth. Thus much for the manner of expression, that "where I am, there you may be also." The latter part is this, that they might be with Christ where He is.

One thing observe: that in Scripture language there is a great difference between Christ's being with us and our being with Christ. That Christ is said to be with us does not denote a personal presence but a presence by His Spirit. Matthew

28:20: "Teaching them to observe all things whatsoever I have commanded you: and lo, I am with you always, even unto the end of the world." It was not in person, for He left them, but "I am with you in My blessings and in My Spirit." But when the Scripture speaks of our being with Christ, it notes being with Christ in person. Therefore Paul says, "I desire to be dissolved and to be with Christ." Christ was with Paul because Christ converted him, but Paul was not with Christ but desired to be dissolved and to be with Christ. Our being with the Lord notes a personal presence, an enjoying of the presence of the Lord.

The Blessedness of Everlasting Communion

The observation is this: that Christ at His second coming receives the elect unto Himself in body and soul, that they might be forever present where Jesus Christ is in heaven. "That where I am, there you may be also." This doctrine is out of the common place. Here in setting out to you that this shall be the consequent of Christ's great and last coming to receive the elect unto Himself, that where Christ is, there ye may be also, I shall show you the great blessedness of this condition in these eight or nine particulars.

First, that you will be more happy in being present with Jesus Christ in heaven than if you had been present with Adam in a state of innocency. We would have thought ourselves happy to be as Adam was, to have had the immediate presence of God; we would have thought this a very happy and glorious estate. Indeed, so it was; but now to be present with Christ in heaven, you are more happy ten thousand times than if you had been made when Adam was made, to have lived with him in inno-cency. [Consider:] (1) Adam, when he was made by God in innocency, he was instated only into an earthly paradise; but now you being with Christ are placed into an everlasting kingdom. (2) Adam was placed in innocency, yet so as to be liable to lose that blessed and glorious condition he was in, and did lose it; though he were a perfect creature, yet he lay under a capacity to lose all his excellency. But when God brings you to be present with Jesus Christ, you are instated into a kingdom that cannot be shaken, into a happy condition that cannot be lost. (3) When he was made by God in innocency, he enjoyed only the society of beasts on the earth and birds of the air; but when God brings you where Christ is, He instates you into a condition where God the Father, God the Son, and all the saints and angels are your companions.

Secondly, here is another part of your happiness by being where Christ is: that you shall enjoy the society of Christ in His human nature. Where Christ is, you shall be. The meaning of that expression is in John 17:24: "Father, I will that they also, whom thou hast given me, be with me where I am; that they may behold my glory." Beloved, this is the beatific vision; this refers to seeing the glory of Christ's person in His human nature, not the glory of His God-head but the glory of His manhood; "that they may behold My glorified body, the glory of My human nature that was so condemned and despised when I was on the earth. Let all the elect that long for Me where I am to behold My glory." It was a solemn wish of Augustine, a little before his death, that he might see three things; and then if he might die, he did not care. "I wish, first," says he, "that I might see Rome in its beauty, and to see Paul in the pulpit, and to see Christ in the flesh." Every believer shall see the Lord Jesus in the flesh. Job tells you of his confidence long before Christ was born: "I know my Redeemer liveth, and with these eyes I shall see my Redeemer." Here is your happiness, that being where Jesus Christ is you have a society with Christ in His human nature, 1 John 3:2: "Beloved, now are we the sons of God, and it doth not yet appear what we shall be: but we know that, when he shall appear, we shall be like him; for we shall see him as he is." We do not know what Christ is; we shall know Him then; we shall see Him as He is glorified in heaven.

A third thing that makes much for the blessedness of the elect, that in your being present with Jesus Christ, God gives you more honor than ever you could be capable of in former times. God gives you glory by virtue of your being with Jesus Christ. A notable text [is] John 12:26: "If any man serve me, let him follow me; and where I am, there shall also my servant be: if any man serve me, him will my Father honour." That is, "where I shall be in heaven." Beloved, the time is now for giving honor to God, and giving glory to God, but your being where Christ is, God then gives you glory and gives you honor.

Fourthly, your happiness in being present with Christ where He is, is that you shall stand in no need of ordinances. Beloved, here the highest grown Christian and the strongest believer in the world stand in more need of ordinances than a lame man does of crutches to go by; but when you come to have this accomplishment, that you shall be where Christ is, you then stand in no need of ordinances than what needs the candlestick of sermons. What needs the candlestick of preaching, and the candlestick of praying, when you are present with Christ, the Sun of Righteousness? There is no need of conduit pipes when you are by the fountain head; you need no ordinances, [for] the conduit pipes are the ordinances. There is no need of ordinances any longer than you are absent from the fountain, which is Jesus Christ. The ceremonial law is all gospel; it is a dark gospel; the evangelists are the explained gospel, the ceremonial law is a dark gospel, Exodus 25. Meaning the holy place. There was to be golden candlesticks which typified the preaching of the Word. In the holy place there was the incense dishes, to wit, Christ's intercession; this was only in the holy place, but in the holy of holiest there was no candlestick, no incense dishes there to show that while you are on this side [of] heaven in the church of God, you need the candlestick; you need preaching and praying. But in the holy of holiest there was none of this to show that it was a type of heaven, and when Christ brings you there, then you are above ordinances, and never till then. This is a fourth particular.

A fifth privilege of your being where Christ is, is that you shall have a full communion and fellowship with Jesus Christ in person. Beloved, here we have our communion with Christ, but it is a communion far different from that which we shall have in heaven: (1) It shall be different in regard of the manner of its enjoyment. In this world, you enjoy Christ mediately by ordinances. You do but see Him (as in the apostle's phrase) in a glass darkly; but in heaven you shall enjoy Christ personally and have communion immediately with Christ in heaven. (2) In regard of the measure of your enjoyment, here you enjoy but a parcel of Christ; you here enjoy Christ's Spirit by drops. You shall then enjoy the fullness of the ocean. (3) It differs in regard of its time and duration. Here you enjoy Christ, it is true, but it is by fits and starts. You enjoy Him now in an ordinance, but you have interrupted fellowship and communion with Christ. But when you are with Him in heaven, there will be no interruption in your communion with Christ. (4) It is different in regard of its expectation: here in heaven you enjoy Christ by way of possession. (5) In regard of place, here there is a great distance between Christ and us. Here we enjoy Christ, He in heaven and we on earth; but then we shall enjoy Christ in one place: He in heaven and we in heaven. Here you may think much of Christ, but if you were nearer Christ, you would see and know more of His glory. (6) There shall be a difference in regard of your companions, and those who are in fellowship with you in heaven are saints and angels, but on earth, though you enjoy Christ, yet you are forced to discourse and commerce with wicked men.

A sixth particular is this, your being present with Jesus Christ, [and] there is this to attend you: there shall be gladness and rejoicing among all the angels in heaven. If the angels in heaven shall rejoice at a sinner's conversion, they shall much rejoice at a sinner's inauguration in heaven. They and we shall make but one fold to glorify the great Shepherd of our souls, the Lord Jesus. What great joy shall there be among angels, archangels, thrones, &c., singing hallelujah to God, making you partners of their glory!

Seventhly, our being with Christ shall put us into a state of exemption from sin—from the causes of sin and from the punishments of sin. (1) From sin; here your beautiful soul is bespotted with the spots of leprosy; I mean with foul and deformed lusts; but when you are with Jesus Christ, you are exempted from sin, no more sin. (2) You shall be exempt from the causes of sin. The devil shall deceive no more there, but here you lie exposed to all temptations. (3) There shall be no more punishments for sin. Here you are punished in your body by diseases and the like; here punishments by trouble of soul, but in heaven you are freed from internal punishments and external punishments.

This was prefigured under the law, 1 Kings 33. The palm tree is an emblem of victory; therefore, the victorious are said to wear palms in their hands triumphing, Revelation 7, to show that you can never be complete conquerors, to wear signals of triumph and signals of conquest in your hands, till you come to enter into the holy of holiest. Then you have conquered over sin, and over temptation to sin, and conquered over all punishments for sin. The moral philosophers say that rain, hail, storm and tempests are engendered in the middle region, but above the middle region there is no wind, no storm or tempest. While you are here below, there are storms, wind, and blustering temptations; but when God takes you above this middle region, there is no storm or tempest to disturb you, but you shall be quiet there.

Eighthly, in being present with Jesus Christ, those who have suffered most, and do most for Jesus Christ, shall have most glory with Jesus Christ. All shall have glory enough. He that has least in heaven shall have enough. Every vessel of glory shall be full, yet some shall contain more than others. As you have had more grace in this world, you shall have more glory.

There are degrees of glory in heaven, and there are degrees of torments in hell; there are degrees and orders among the angels in heaven, not only angels, but archangels, not only cherubims and seraphims but distinct orders among angels. There surely is an order and degree among glorified saints, that those that have done most for Christ, and suffered most for Christ, shall have most glory from Jesus Christ. It is the saying of one that as God communicates His graces in an unequal manner in this life, so He shall crown them in an unequal manner in the life to come. As you have gone beyond some men in graces, so you shall be beyond some men in glory in enjoying the bodily presence of Jesus Christ.

[Ninthly,] you shall know all the bodies of all your well-beloved friends that you know here in the world; this most divines do concur in. Bolton[1] is very strong for it; all our modern authors are for it, and some of the ancients too. I only give it as a probable advantage and comfort. Then a man shall say, "Here is the child that I sought God for"; and may the minister say, "Here are the people that I have preached to"; and the people say, "Here is the minister now in heaven that I have heard."

Take these probable grounds for it. First, that the wicked knew the godly in heaven. Dives in hell knew Lazarus in heaven. Then we read likewise in Luke 13:28: "There shall be weeping and gnashing of teeth, when ye shall see Abraham, and Isaac, and Jacob, and all the prophets, in the kingdom of God, and you

---

1. Robert Bolton (1572–1631), English Puritan clergyman noted for his intellectual acumen and teachings on spiritual comfort. Love here refers to Bolton's discussion in *Mr. Bolton's Last and Learned Work of the Four Last Things, Death, Judgment, Heaven, and Hell* (1639), 144–50.

yourselves thrust out." Now if the damned in hell see Abraham, Isaac, and Jacob in the kingdom of God, why shall not the godly know one another there? Then again, Peter, James, and John knew Moses in the transfiguration, Matthew 13. Then again, the godly knew the damned in hell; therefore, certainly, they know one another in heaven. It is said in Matthew 8:11: "And I say unto you, That many shall come from the east and west, and shall sit down with Abraham, and Isaac, and Jacob, in the kingdom of heaven." I do not give you this for certain; I am loath in things controversial, tossed to and fro by learned men, rashly to determine; but there are strong hints to build hopes on that in your knowing Christ in person, and when the bodies of the elect shall be raised, you shall know the bodies of your elect friends. Bolton here thinks it should detract much from the happiness of every saint in heaven if every saint should not know one another which knew one another here upon earth. This adds much for the adjuncts of this condition, that "where Christ is, there ye may be also."

Applications of Everlasting Communion

The use then. If it is so that where Jesus Christ is, that place where He is gone to heaven, there you shall be also, then I infer [this]: take well at Christ's hand whatever you have here below. Suppose you live in a smoky cottage; suppose you have not a place to put your head. O think what a place Christ has gone to prepare for you! He has gone to prepare no worse a place for you than heaven. Nay, be content with a prison; be content with a dungeon; the place in heaven shall make a recompense for all the obscure places in the world. Suppose you be as Christ was in the world, that the foxes have holes, and the birds of the air have nests, but the Son of Man has nowhere to lay His head. But He has a house in heaven, a house not made with hands, a building of God. He has His Father's house in heaven. There you may go.

You must be patient. Though the places you dwell in are not as comfortable as you may desire, you shall be where Jesus Christ is.

Secondly, if it be so that it is the great benefit of Christ's coming again to take us to Himself, to be in the same place where He is, then take heed that you be not so foolish as to lose a place in heaven for worldly profits and preferments, for earth to lose heaven. It is the great bait of these times to have places, and preferments, and advantages. Take heed they do not make you lose the place in heaven where Christ is. Historians that write of Tiberius[2] stigmatize him for a very fool that would for a drop of drink sell his kingdom, and so [it] was called of Tiberius, "Biberius."[3] O there are many such Biberius's in the world, that for a draught of drink will venture the danger of drinking down shovels full of fire to their own damnation. Many in the world that will rather than lose their places and possessions here upon earth, venture to lose that place where Jesus Christ is.

Thus I have in ten sermons finished five main points of religion. "And if I go and prepare a place for you, I will come again, and receive you unto myself; that where I am, there ye may be also."

---

2. Tiberius Caesar Augustus (42 BC–AD 37), the second Roman emperor and adopted son of Augustus, known for his tyrannical reign in his latter years.

3. Biberius: "bibulous," or "drink loving."